Barry B. Bridger

The Spirit to Soar

Jim Petersen

JIM PETERSEN, PhD

**The True Story of
Former Orphan & POW,
Lt. Col. Barry B. Bridger,
US Air Force (Ret)**

The SPIRIT to SOAR

Inspiring Life Lessons and Values for a Victorious Life

NEW YORK

LONDON • NASHVILLE • MELBOURNE • VANCOUVER

The Spirit to Soar

Inspiring Life Lessons and Values for a Victorious Life (The True Story of Former Orphan and POW, Lt. Col. Barry B. Bridger, US Air Force (Ret))

Published in New York, New York, by Morgan James Publishing. Morgan James is a trademark of Morgan James, LLC. www.MorganJamesPublishing.com

Proudly distributed by Ingram Publisher Services.

The cover photo of Barry Bridger in a homecoming parade with an American flag and the photo of Bridger in a homecoming parade in chapter 12 are used with permission from the *Bladen Journal*, Elizabethtown, North Carolina.

Morgan James BOGO™

A **FREE** ebook edition is available for you or a friend with the purchase of this print book.

CLEARLY SIGN YOUR NAME ABOVE

Instructions to claim your free ebook edition:
1. Visit MorganJamesBOGO.com
2. Sign your name CLEARLY in the space above
3. Complete the form and submit a photo of this entire page
4. You or your friend can download the ebook to your preferred device

ISBN 9781631956515 case laminate
ISBN 9781631956522 ebook
Library of Congress Control Number: 2021938980

Cover & Interior Design by:
Christopher Kirk
www.GFSstudio.com

Morgan James PUBLISHING **Builds** with... **Habitat for Humanity** Peninsula and Greater Williamsburg

Morgan James is a proud partner of Habitat for Humanity Peninsula and Greater Williamsburg. Partners in building since 2006.

Get involved today! Visit MorganJamesPublishing.com/giving-back

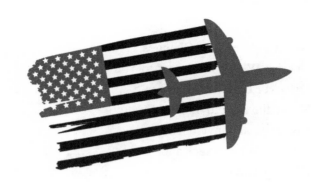

TABLE OF CONTENTS

Acknowledgments vii

Foreword by John M. (Mike) McGrath, Captain, USN (Ret.) ix

Preface xiii

Introduction xv

Chapter 1   Face Your Fears to Build Courage. 1

Chapter 2   Find What Makes You Thankful 5

Chapter 3   Adopt Values That Will Guide Your Future Decisions 25

Chapter 4   Stand on the Shoulders of Those Who Came Before You 37

Chapter 5   Hope for the Best, but Prepare for the Worst. 45

Chapter 6   Gain Wisdom from Failure 51

Chapter 7   Keep Your Sense of Humor, No Matter What 63

Chapter 8   Always Look for New Ways to Do Things 77

Chapter 9   Hold to Your Values to Overcome Your
Greatest Challenges. 85

Chapter 10 Make Every Day a Good Day by Controlling Your Mind. . . .95

Chapter 11 Learn Patience as a Powerful Tool for Success 103

Chapter 12   Adapt as Your Life Changes 119
Chapter 13   Cherish What's Important to You .135
Chapter 14   Discover Unconditional Love 157
Chapter 15   Know the Source of Your Strength 167
Chapter 16   Constantly Reinvent Yourself 185
Chapter 17   Live by Your Virtues and Values. .197
Chapter 18   Closing Thoughts 205
Conclusion: The Meaning of Life 211

More about Barry Bridger 215
About Jim Petersen 221

ACKNOWLEDGMENTS

Many thanks to my wonderful wife, Louise, and my children—Jackie Keane, Greg Petersen, and Matt Petersen—for having the patience to let their husband and father work tirelessly over the years on projects such as this one.

Thank you to Sheila Bridger, Barry's wife, for her expert help in relating historical information about Barry and maintaining her endless enthusiasm as we worked on this book. Barry and Sheila's daughters, Deidra Johnson and Courtney Isernhagen, were a great help in reflecting on growing up with their American-hero father.

Thank you to John M. (Mike) McGrath, Captain, US Navy (Ret.), who got to know Barry when he spent five years and eight months as a POW in North Vietnam prison camps. Not only did Mike provide valuable insight; he also demonstrated enthusiasm for the book. He generously wrote the foreword and gave us permission to use one of the compelling illustrations from his book, *Prisoner of War—Six Years in Hanoi*, with his foreword.

Thank you to Libbye Morris for her vision and expertise in keeping me on track for developing my first three books. Libbye is the kind of teammate all writers need.

Thank you to Dennis Welch, publicist, who gave me the insight to focus this book on "lessons learned." His inspiration is just what I needed to finish the book.

Thank you also to Barry's and my colleagues whom we interviewed about their experiences during the Vietnam War and their colorful recollections about Barry through the years. Their commentary does not appear in this book but will appear in other related venues:

- Rich Giles, entrepreneur; Barry's former boss; Senior Vice President for Advisor Operations at Barry's financial services company
- Ron Huff, Colonel, US Air Force reconnaissance officer, retired
- Doug Petersen, Chief Warrant Officer 4, US Army helicopter pilot, retired
- Lamar Smith, CEO of Barry's financial services company; former US Air Force Search and Rescue Pilot
- Dick Terrell, Colonel, US Army, retired
- Doris Terrell, military wife and mother

FOREWORD

June 30, 1967, would be the fateful day that began my introduction to a lifelong friendship with Barry Bridger. I was shot down over North Vietnam, destined to endure a five-year, eight-month ordeal as a POW in the Hanoi Hilton. Little did I know that a young US Air Force Captain, a future friend, had preceded me by almost exactly six months.

Our captors had plenty of practice torturing Barry, and then they repeated their lessons learned on me and the other 500+ pilots and air crew captured in North Vietnam. We later learned that 28 of our fellow pilots had died in torture in the prisons of Hanoi. Barry and I survived.

One cannot imagine the fear and anguish of being alone in the hands of a brutal enemy who is torturing you to betray your country with radio statements or false written confessions. There is no hope…rescue will never come. You will die fearing that your family will never know your fate. Then, from within a brick wall, comes the "shave and a haircut" rhythm of a knocking sound. You know it must be an American on the other side.

With time, POWs learned the tap code that saved our sanity and gave us the will to resist. Yes, it was Barry Bridger and men like him who had the courage and the leadership to risk all to reassure a helpless, wounded fellow pilot. At the time, that summer of 1967, I had lain helpless for one month, covered with boils, skin infections, and thousands of itching mosquito bites. With a broken arm, four joint dislocations, and a back injured by compression fractures, I was unable to sit up or lift my head. No medical help was ever rendered. You either lived or died.

My spirit had been broken. Then it came…that soft yet recognizable rhythmic knock on the wall: "shave and a haircut." Barry and I would continue to communicate with each other and with the other POWs in isolated cells for the next five years, never seeing the face of another American.

Barry has his own words and descriptions on how he was able to survive, but I remember most how he taught me to survive. He taught me his "three C's," which were easy to remember when under extreme stress. First, depend on the strength of your own *character*, which you have developed since childhood and carried throughout your life. Never waver. Second, have the *courage* to make the decision to resist—to resist again and again and never give in to the enemy. Finally, the hard choice: make the *commitment* to carry through with your hard decision to endure untold misery and fear that lie ahead. Have faith—this, too, shall pass.

Barry set the example for all of us: "No matter what they do to us, no matter what we endure, our goal is to *return with honor*." We did it.

We formed unbreakable bonds of friendship. We returned to our families. We continued to serve our country. We served with pride and honor.

Thank you, Barry, for showing me the way.

John M. (Mike) McGrath, Captain, USN (Ret.)
Author, *Prisoner of War—Six Years in Hanoi*

From My Book: The "Vietnamese Rope Trick":[1]

Here, I tried to depict the "Vietnamese rope trick." The arms are repeatedly clinched up until the elbows are forced together. Sometimes at this point the "hell cuffs" are applied. The "hell cuffs" are handcuffs which are put on the upper arms and pinched as tightly as possible onto the arms, cutting off the circulation. The resulting pain is extreme. If the prisoner has not broken down by this time, his arms are rotated until the shoulders dislocate. Words could never adequately describe the pain, or the thoughts that go through a man's mind at a time like this.

1 John M. McGrath, Captain, US Navy (Ret.), *Prisoner of War—Six Years in Hanoi* (Annapolis, Maryland: Naval Institute Press, 1975), 78–79.

PREFACE

With many books, you must read all the way to the end to discover the most important nugget of wisdom in the story.

This book is different.

What we all need to know—and what Lt. Col. Barry B. Bridger, US Air Force (Ret.) will tell you with the utmost conviction—is that when you find yourself in imminent danger, you will be all alone with your thoughts and your values. And those values will save you, no matter the danger that lurks ahead or the challenges you face.

As you read Barry's inspiring story of perseverance, faith, and courage, think about your own values and how they inform your everyday life. Are those values compelling enough and ingrained deeply enough to sustain you through a situation in which, like Barry, you are captured by a savage enemy and subjected to years of torture? Are your values such that you can make it through the inevitable tough times that we all face periodically that make it hard to continue?

Jesus said that in this world, we *will* have trouble. He didn't say *might*. It comes for all of us, and most of the time, it catches us unaware, with no warning. Now is the time to prepare. Your values will be your shock absorbers when trouble comes, but you must be proactive and put them in place *now*. They can come from your parents, your church, your school, and your true friends. Spend your life finding a life partner and good friends who have your best interests at heart. The best of them will change you for good and strengthen you.

Most importantly, find wisdom wherever you can find it. On these pages, Lt. Col. Barry Bridger shares with you the wisdom he gained from his experiences as an orphan and a survivor of more than six years of confinement in a North Vietnamese prison camp. My hope is that his story will be as life changing for you as it has been for me.

The American Vietnam prisoner of war experience is not a story about the plight of American POWs serving in the prison camps of Vietnam nearly so much as it is a revelation of the power of traditional American values." —Lt. Col. Barry B. Bridger (Ret.)

INTRODUCTION

Jim

The inspiration for this book came to me many years ago after I first met Barry Bridger. He attended my training classes to become a financial advisor.

This retired US Air Force officer was different. He came across like an unguided missile, full of energy and fascinated with life and human behavior. Barry stood out from the others I trained over the years, whether in the US Navy or the financial services industry. I didn't know why at the time, but we became close friends.

Likely, it was because Barry is an outlier. As Malcolm Gladwell shares in his book *Outliers: The Story of Success*, it takes 10,000 hours to master anything. As you will find out in this book, Barry spends 10,000 hours or more mastering anything he feels is important in life.

Since I first met Barry many years ago, my family and his family have become remarkably close. Barry's delightful wife, Sheila, navigated the skies as a flight attendant with Delta Airlines for forty-six years. Sheila shows the same zest for life that Barry shows. The Chili Queen from Luckenbach, Texas, met her match in Barry after he returned from Vietnam, and they have a wonderful marriage.

Over the years, I watched the Bridger girls, Deidra and Courtney, develop into young ladies and great wives and mothers. Barry raised them around what could be considered traditional male outdoor activities, such as hunting and fishing. His daughters love those activities to this day, and they are quite accomplished in all they do.

So why write this book? I don't recall the actual moment when I decided to do so, but more than fifteen years ago, I realized that I didn't know the full Barry Bridger story. Like others, I heard many of Barry's stories about being a prisoner of war in Vietnam. That horrific experience certainly commanded him the respect of an American hero, and I wanted to know more about what made Barry do what he does.

One night, when I was with Barry and Sheila, I asked Barry to share his story about growing up, leading up to the moment his F-4 Phantom was shot down over Hanoi in North Vietnam. I was amazed at how much I did not know about this man and how he developed into the person he is today.

At that time, I asked Sheila and Barry's permission to write his biography so others could learn the immeasurable value of this human success story called Barry Bridger. I also felt that others needed to know the life lessons that come from Barry's pursuit of excellence.

It was not easy for Barry, but having Sheila by his side after he returned to the United States helped him transition back into American life. Barry spent his time during incarceration as a bachelor.

As we collected information for this book, Barry continually reminded us that this story is not about him—it's about the people who influenced him in his life. I agree with that. I also agree that understanding the difficulty of his early life in an orphanage will inspire others to overcome the difficulties in their own lives.

It is important to understand how each phase of Barry's early life contributed to his development and future success. It is a great story of triumph as he worked through different phases. In the first phase of his life, he was an orphan. In the second phase, he was adopted, and in the third phase, he grew up in a loving family, which included the journey to virtue brought on by a solid upbringing built on ethics and values. This strong foundation helped him through the most difficult times during incarceration in North Vietnam. He came out a changed man who was able to inspire others, as he has me.

After his adoption, Barry's life and values continued to be molded through his career as a fighter pilot in the military, his experiences in Vietnam, incarceration and torture in the "Hanoi Hilton," a successful business and speaking career, and reinvention of himself as an accomplished musician and singer—an in-process endeavor.

This is an inspirational journey. I hope it will inspire you to put your own troubles in life in perspective as you learn about Barry's. His life serves as an inspiration to us all to find meaning in our own lives.

It has been said that as iron sharpens iron, so one person sharpens another. Barry Bridger has sharpened me. He has shown me how to deal with the worst kind of adversity and come through it with the most upbeat, positive, and resilient attitude I have ever witnessed.

Because of my association with Barry Bridger over the years, I, like others, have learned many life lessons that helped me deal with how to work through this maze called life. I consider myself to be privileged because I was the recipient of Barry sharing with me what he has experienced in life and what it means to others.

I accompany Barry in fireside chats to communicate to others what he has endured. He reminds me constantly that this is not about him but about others who are faced with challenges in their lives. He is an inspiration and a humble human being.

Recently, I read a blog post titled "137 Powerful Life Lessons Everyone Should Learn."[2] As I read those life lessons, I saw some that mirror the lessons Barry Bridger has learned in his life. I want to thank the author(s) of that article for helping me come up with the ones that apply to Barry.

---

2   "137 Powerful Life Lessons Everyone Should Learn," DevelopGoodHabits.com, https://www.developgoodhabits.com/life-lessons/.

We can learn much from other people's hard-earned wisdom. I hope you glean as much wisdom from Barry's story as I have.

I hope you enjoy *The Spirit to Soar*.

This book is dedicated to the Bridger family: Barry, Sheila, Deidra, and Courtney—the team that made the book possible.

Chapter 1

FACE YOUR FEARS
TO BUILD COURAGE

Jim

The first lesson Barry taught me early on was that facing fear head-on breeds courage. There is no other way to live a strong life. To develop the kind of courage that is prevalent in our heroes and that we have revered through history, we must be placed in fearful situations in which the outcome is uncertain. As you read Barry Bridger's tale about a harrowing and life-changing event, think about how you would react in a similar situation.

Barry

On January 23, 1967, my copilot, Dave Grey, and I launched a mission in our F-4 Phantom fighter jet in treacherous weather. It was my seventy-fifth mission and the only daytime mission I ever attempted.

Every 2,000 feet, we hit a deck of clouds. We were flying in the clear 4,000 feet above the last deck of clouds. That's the last place you want to be because when a missile comes out of the clouds, as fast as those SA-2 missiles were able to fly, you have only seconds to dodge or detect the missile. At least I knew to look left 10 o'clock and left 8 o'clock for possible surface-to-air (SAM) missile activity. Suddenly I saw a glow coming up through the clouds at left 10 o'clock. I hit my mic button and said, "Bobcat flight break left, SAM 10 o'clock low."

We had been briefed to not take evasive action but trust the pod. After I called the missile out to the rest of the flight, we started a gentle turn, maintaining "pod formation." I did not see the second missile coming from left 8 o'clock. I became quite anxious. A gentle turn didn't make sense, and my aircraft had no pod. So I flipped upside down and pulled straight down toward the Earth.

Then I heard an explosion.

Due to the impact of the missile and the aircraft coming apart, all the warning lights in the cockpit lit up. There are a lot of caution lights in a fighter aircraft. I was somewhat mesmerized by all the lights clicking on at once. I don't think I'd ever seen them. I looked at my dash panel, and all those lights lit up. It said, "You need to service your hydraulic reservoir. Your oil pressure's low on the right engine. Your left engine is overheating. Your right engine is on fire."

Then one light that I had never seen came on that said, "You're in deep kimchi."

Then the stick went limp, and fire was everywhere. Captain Dave Grey, my copilot, figured I was dead, so he ejected. I didn't even know he left the aircraft. I never heard him go. Meanwhile, I was sitting there looking at all those lights, still going about 600 miles an hour, true air speed. With the wings and tail gone, the aircraft was spinning uncontrollably through the air. I reached for the ejection handle unsuccessfully due to the torque created by my rapidly spinning aircraft. Then my adrenaline kicked in, and my second effort was successful. I said to myself, "It is going to be very breezy."

I shut my eyes, pulled the handle, and ejected from the aircraft. It was breezy as heck, and when I opened my eyes, I was blind. I said, "Oh, great.

Now I can't see." I grabbed at my face and discovered, to my great joy, that my helmet had spun around on my head, and I was looking into the back of the helmet. I turned it around and said, "Yes! I can see!"

Shrapnel had hit my helmet and loosened it enough to spin it around on my head. The shrapnel had also left a deep cut in the top of my skull, which was bleeding profusely.

I left the aircraft sitting in the ejection seat. Upon ejection, a chute attached to the seat is deployed to stabilize it and allows it to descend at a controlled rate of speed of about 80 miles per hour. A pressure sensor on the seat detects when you hit 10,000 feet pressure altitude, automatically kicks you out of the seat, and deploys your main parachute so you can safely descend to the Earth.

The clouds that day were layered about every 2,000 feet, and each layer was about 500 feet thick. I couldn't see the ground. I was just falling through decks of clouds—*thump, thump, thump*. I was also looking up at the altitude sensor on the side of the seat, saying to myself, "That sucker had better work because, eventually, there's going to be dirt in one of these decks of clouds."

After a while, my mathematical mind cranked up and I thought, "Well, let me calculate how far I've fallen. I'm falling at about 125 feet per second and I guess I have been falling for about 80 seconds, which means I have fallen about 10,000 feet. I ejected at 20,000 feet. So why hasn't my main chute deployed?"

At that moment, I lost all confidence in the pressure sensor. I decided to manually separate from the ejection seat and deploy my main chute myself. I reached down and pulled a handle that would release me and my main parachute from the ejection seat. Now it was up to me to pull my parachute handle, my ripcord to inflate my parachute, and safely descend to the Earth. In other words, I no longer had an automatic system to deploy my main parachute.

The instant I pulled that handle and the seat sped away from me, I saw a strap fly up over my head. Instinctively, I reached up and grabbed it. Now I was free falling at about 125 miles an hour, looking at that strap that was hooked to a bag about 9 feet over my head. It dawned on me that the bag had to be my chute, but I couldn't figure out why it was nine feet over my head.

So I pulled the bag down to my hands. But initially, I still could not find a handle to deploy my chute. Within moments, I did find the handle attached to my right shoulder harness, where it belonged. So I pulled it. Of course, the chute opened right there in front of my eyes and snapped me—dang near broke my back. I learned later you don't want to deploy the chute close to your body because when it inflates, it can break your back as it snaps open with the air. You really want it up above you, completely extended, to avoid injury.

I did it the wrong way. I deployed my own chute manually, after I had ejected from the aircraft. That's probably one of the reasons my back has been injured ever since. But we never practiced ejecting from aircraft. I did what came naturally to me in the moment.

I don't know if anyone else has ever done what I did. Most people rely on automatic deployment when they eject. Of course, most people fly in a non-weather environment. Mine was a very severe-weather environment, and that complicated the whole process. It would have been much easier if I had been able to see the ground. But 2,000 feet below me was another deck of clouds. Who knows what it was hiding? I didn't know.

During that incredible event, I was busy trying to figure out how to do things. It never crossed my mind that anything was going to happen other than the fact that I needed to pay attention to what I was going to do next. I was completely engaged in my attempts to monitor my descent and survive my parachute opening.

I had no idea of the nightmare that was waiting for me. What happened next was a defining moment that completely altered the trajectory of my life.

Chapter 2

FIND WHAT MAKES YOU THANKFUL

Jim

As the second-oldest child in a family that eventually had eleven children—seven boys and four girls—I had to help out with my siblings a lot. We were privileged to have a loving mother and father who made sure we were cared for. For many in America, this is a relatively normal upbringing, except for all those siblings.

I am most thankful to my parents and my siblings for helping define who I would eventually become. When I asked Barry to discuss the early part of his life, I found that our upbringings were quite different. Barry's early childhood wasn't ideal, but it led to a life that he is now thankful for—and it helped mold him into the brave, resilient person those of us who know him are thankful for.

Barry
Pea Soup, Billy, and Watching Cars Pull Up to the Orphanage

On July 16, 1940, I came into this world in Durham, North Carolina. Durham is the home for some great institutions of higher learning, which is likely why my life began as it did.

The first moment I knew I was on the Earth was when I saw a lot of shade, brown and green paint, and a toilet. Those are the first things I remember seeing. I was an orphan and practically a baby. In the Durham County Orphanage, we all ate together at long tables. We seemed to eat nothing but green-pea soup. I don't like soup much, and I dang sure don't like green peas, so I spent a lot of my time running to the commode and throwing up. So that is how my life got started.

It had to get better.

It did. The second memory I have is of a little boy named Billy, who was about my age. We hit it off and became friends in that orphanage at a very early age. We quickly discovered that without helping one another, we had access to nothing that kids normally receive in large quantities—toys. There were no toys. When we were lucky to find a ball or a bat, the older kids took them, so we were constantly in a big war with the older kids. We played with anything we could find to play with.

Billy and I generally spent most of our time underneath an old chinaberry tree, which was outside the orphanage where the automobile pathway led up to the main building. We sat there and basically just talked to each other because we did not have much to play with. We cut up and laughed at each other to pass the time.

My third memory was cars pulling up in front of the orphanage on that circular driveway. Billy and I sat there and watched those cars; it became a sort of entertainment because I had never ridden in a car. The cars pulled up, and the doors opened. People got out, all dressed up, and walked into the front door of the orphanage.

Putting Up with Ellis the Bully So I Could Ride in a Car

Billy and I sat there and speculated about what was going on. We weren't sure, but we really enjoyed watching those cars pull up. Then one day, this car pulled up, and the back door opened. A little boy about my age got out. His name was Ellis. He was kind of a big boy for his age. The first time he stepped out of that car and looked at me, I immediately didn't like him. He felt the same about me. We didn't need to say a word to figure that out. He walked into the front door of the orphanage with two people I assumed were his father and his mother.

Billy and I were talking about the car, the people who got out, and what might be going on. About that time, the door to the orphanage opened, and out came the headmaster, who walked over to me and said, "Barry, come with me."

I walked into the orphanage, and there stood Ellis with his parents. The headmaster said, "Barry, would you like to go with the Spake family and spend the night?"

It took me a while to realize what they were asking, but I said, "Absolutely."

The reason I said yes was to get my first ride in their car. I could deal with Ellis because I definitely wanted to get in that car. So we all got in and went to their home. We ate cottontail rabbit for supper. Let me tell you, if you cook cottontail rabbits correctly, they are delicious, just like chicken. That was my first taste of bunny rabbit.

I spent the night. The next morning, I was up before anybody because I was absolutely mesmerized with everything I saw in the house. I had never been in a home, so I had not seen stoves or garages. Out in front of the house was a goldfish pond, about ten feet across. It had a lot of goldfish in it. I'd never seen a pond and dang sure had never seen a goldfish.

I was just sitting there awed by life, which was unfurling for me at a rapid pace. At that moment, Ellis came out and walked over to the goldfish pond. He reached down and grabbed one of the goldfish. I could tell that he was squeezing the goldfish, and I didn't like that. I immediately reacted, and I knocked it out of his hand. We got into a big fight right there in the front yard.

Hearing Ellis and me scuffling, Mr. Spake came running out just as I pushed Ellis's head under the water in that goldfish pond. But Ellis was a pretty strong kid, so he didn't drown. Mr. Spake grabbed me by the cuff of the neck, lifted me up, set me down, lifted me up again, and set me down again. That afternoon, the Spakes took me back to the orphanage.

My first experience in the real world turned out poorly.

Billy Leaves Forever

Then I was back underneath the chinaberry tree with Billy, and I didn't expect to ever see the Spake family again.

About six months later, another car pulled up. A couple got out and walked into the orphanage. Not long thereafter, the headmaster came out, walked over to the chinaberry tree where Billy and I were, and said, "Billy, come with me."

Billy walked off with the headmaster into the orphanage, and within a short period of time, the couple came out with Billy. He got into the car, and they drove off. I never saw him again. The only friend I had in the world had left. At a very young age, I was all alone.

The days turned into weeks and months, and it was just me under the chinaberry tree. I was doing OK overall, but time was going by very slowly.

And then one day, a car pulled up. I didn't recognize the automobile, but it was the Spake family again, with Ellis. They went inside, and not long thereafter, the headmaster came outside, took me back into the orphanage, and said, "Barry, the Spake family would like to take you on a trip. They're going to drive from Durham, North Carolina, down to a little town called Bladenboro, North Carolina. They're going to spend the weekend down there with friends. Would you like to go with them?"

Well, absolutely I did. That meant I'd be able to have a ride in that car again.

Banned from the Front Seat

I jumped into the car. We drove to their home, and they put some items in the car. By that time, it was late in the evening. We got on the road and started driving south. I was in the front passenger seat. Mrs. Spake was driving. Mr. Spake and Ellis were in the backseat, and within an hour, they were both sound asleep.

As darkness fell, a whole new world opened before my eyes. I had never seen lights on the inside of a car, and I'd never watched headlights in the distance as they appeared and then disappeared. Everything was a new experience. Going across a bridge in a car was something I'd never done. I couldn't stop looking outside at all the wildlife, the forest, and the rivers. I'd never seen any of those things, so I was very alert, experiencing as much as I could.

It started raining, and Mrs. Spake turned on the windshield wipers, which was another new experience for me. I was captivated, watching the wipers slide back and forth across the windshield. I was particularly interested in all the lights on the dash panel. She was driving about 55 miles per hour down a country road, and it was about 9:00 at night. I couldn't contain myself. I saw an interesting-looking button and pushed it. When I did, the headlights went off. Pandemonium exploded. The tires squealed loudly, and I knew I'd done something wrong. As the car came to a screeching halt, I pulled my arms back and tried to hide on the passenger side of the front seat.

Of course, Mr. Spake and Ellis woke up, and they thought they were dead, I guess. I was instructed to get in the backseat. From then on, I was a backseat rider as we traveled to the home of the Hillburn family. It turned out that the Hillburns were really nice folks down there in little old Bladenboro, North Carolina. They were good friends with the Spakes, although I don't recall how that friendship started. The Hillburn family invited the Spake family down to spend the weekend. I don't remember what the occasion was, but I was all game to do it, that's for sure. This was my first opportunity to experience family life outside the orphanage.

How a Birthday Party Changed My Life

During the conversation the grown-ups had that evening, I learned that there was a little girl in town by the name of Nanette Fussel, who was my age, and she was having a birthday party the next day. Mrs. Hillburn said, "Well, why don't we call the Fussel family because I'm sure they'd love for Barry to go to the birthday party. He and Nanette are the same age."

That was my first opportunity to attend a birthday party.

Arrangements were made, and the next afternoon, Mrs. Hillburn drove me to the Fussel home. As I stepped out of the car, I saw eight or ten kids standing around, and they were blowing on those little blowout party favors. They would blow into the rolled-up paper tubes, which would make a honking noise as they unfurled. I had never seen one of them. When I stepped out, all the kids came up and started blowing those tubes in my face. I immediately became irritated and struck back in a hostile way, which I'd learned to do in the orphanage. That, for me, was a way of life. Mrs. Nettie Van, Nanette's mother, immediately shooed the kids back, so this encounter did not end up like the earlier one with Ellis and the fishpond. She grabbed me by the hand and said, "Barry, would you like some ice cream and cake?"

Now, I did know what ice cream and cake were, and I darn sure wanted some. I said, "Yes, ma'am."

Mrs. Nettie Van cut a piece of cake, dished up some ice cream in a bowl, and handed it to me with a spoon. From daily life at the orphanage, I had a lot of experience finding a private place to eat. I looked around and saw a mimosa tree in full bloom. I breathed in that rich fragrance that only a mimosa gives off in the springtime. I walked over to the mimosa tree, which was about thirty yards from the other kids. They were all doing their own thing, and I was happy they were. I sat down, leaned against that tree, and started eating my ice cream and cake.

When I finally looked up, I gazed across the street. In front of my eyes was an incredibly beautiful home with six stately columns and a slate walkway leading up to the front door. A big magnolia tree in full bloom stood on the left side of the walkway, and the lawn was adorned with azaleas and camellias, all in full bloom. It was another first, a picture I had never seen in my life. I was fascinated with the home, the lawn, and everything I saw. In fact, I was so fascinated that I quit eating my ice cream and cake.

At that moment, Nettie Van, the hostess of the birthday party, said, "Barry, would you like to go over and see that home?"

It was as if she was reading my mind. I said, "Yes, ma'am. I really would."

She took me by the hand, and we walked across the street, around to the side door of the home. We were met there by a lady, who Nettie Van introduced me to as Miss Myrtle. Miss Myrtle said, "Barry, why don't you come on in and just run around and look at anything you wish? If you want anything, just come back, and we'll help you out. We'll be here in this room."

She did not squeeze my cheeks; she did not ask me to sit down and talk to her. She said, "Go do anything you want to do. We'll be in here if you need us." That felt good. I launched down the hallway, which was covered in red velvet carpet. Every room I passed fascinated me.

While exploring the home, I saw a stairwell, so I walked up the stairs. I wasn't afraid to be adventuresome. Everything was amazing, so I just kept going. Then I heard what I knew was a radio. I'd heard that sound a few times. I've always been attracted to sound, and as I walked into the room where the sound was coming from, I interrupted a gentleman who was lying on a bed reading the evening paper. His name was Mr. Henry.

As I walked into the room, he heard my footsteps. He dropped the paper so he could look at me. He immediately, without hesitation, picked the paper back up, placed it back in front of his eyes, and said, "It's the Yankees and the Tigers. The score is six to five in favor of the Yankees. If you want to hear the game, sit down on that other bed over there."

Mr. Henry didn't say another word to me. He kept on reading. By his action, he disarmed any tendency I had to be afraid or hesitant. I sat down on the other bed, and I said one thing: "I hope the Yankees win. I don't like tigers."

As soon as the game ended, Mr. Henry said, "OK, it's the Yankees. They won the game." He never lowered his newspaper again. I got up and walked down the hallway and back down the stairs.

The Wonderful Miss Maggie and Her Fabulous Cooking

My next experience came as I walked down another hallway. I could smell cooking. I walked into the kitchen. I was moving fast, and I walked straight into a lady by the name of Maggie Swindell Jones. She was a beautiful black American lady. I had never seen a black American lady, so I was startled. She looked just like Aunt Jemima, with a scarf around her head.

I felt like maybe I should not be there, so I turned around and started to run out of the kitchen. She said, "Where are you going? You come on back here. Don't call me Maggie. Call me Mum a jug i e so swack i nono du d love love."

I had no idea what that was all about, but that is the name she used for herself: "Mum a jug jug i e so swack i nono du d love love." I walked back into the kitchen because she completely disarmed me when she said that. Then she said, "Come on in here. I have something for you. You ever had peach cobbler?"

I didn't know what she was talking about, so I said, "No."

She said, "Come here." She dished me up some peach cobbler, right off the stove, with some ice cream. I thought I'd died and gone to heaven. She said, "Don't you tell anybody you got that cobbler."

I said, "I'm not going to say a word."

"You want some more?"

Of course I did. I will never forget that experience as long as I live. What a wonderful, wonderful lady. What a wonderful, wonderful experience. She was Myrtle and Henry's maid, and she had her own apartment on the same property.

After I finished eating my peach cobbler, I walked to the other end of the house, where Miss Myrtle and Nettie Van were. It was time for supper. Nettie Van got up and left. Miss Myrtle said, "Barry would you like to eat supper and spend the night with Mr. Henry and me?"

"Yes, ma'am."

We walked back into an eating area attached to the kitchen and sat down. I ate supper with the Bridger family, and darned if I didn't get peach cobbler again. Things were looking up in a big way.

By the time we finished supper, it was about 8:00 p.m. We did some things around the house, and after some time passed, Miss Myrtle said to me, "Barry, I want to show you where you're going to spend the night."

We walked up the stairwell, and she opened a door I had missed earlier. We walked into a room that had a propeller on the ceiling. The room had a balcony attached to it and a private bathroom. Aircraft paraphernalia was displayed all around the room. Mr. Henry and Miss Myrtle's son, McRae, was a World War II aviator, flying P-51 Mustangs in the South Pacific, as well as P-40 Thunderbolts and P-38s. He was quite an aviator, quite an

American hero. This room had been his room, as he grew up. I went to bed under a propeller, and all those aviation artifacts, in a world I could have never imagined.

Jim

As you can tell from Barry's story, he lost all he had in the world when Billy got adopted.

But through persistence and determination—and some divine intervention—Barry's life became one that made it easy for him to be thankful. Based on his adventurous spirit, I wonder if the Bridgers knew what they were getting themselves into when they adopted this young, precocious, curious boy. I know that Barry was thankful for the Bridgers, and I am sure that, with time, the Bridgers were thankful to have him in their lives, too. Barry was a bit of a challenge, as you will see.

Barry
My Big Adventure: Lost for Two Days at Age Five

At about 3:00 in the morning that first night at Myrtle and Henry's home, I woke up, wide awake. I put on my clothes, walked downstairs, opened the door, and walked outside. I was five years old. There were two streets in Bladenboro—a front street and a back street, parallel to each other. Their house was on Front Street. I walked out to the street and began walking down the road.

Every hundred yards or so, there was a new adventure. I could hardly take in all the new sounds, sights, and smells I was experiencing for the first time. It was unending stimulation as I walked along, just looking, listening, smelling, and touching everything. When daylight broke, the Bridger family discovered I was gone. They called the local sheriff, who immediately summoned the highway patrol and the Wildlife Department. The citizens of that small community also joined in the search for the lost orphan—me!

By the time darkness fell, I was still wild and free. I was five to seven miles down country road after country road in an area that was dense with heavy foliage. The various search groups became concerned about this little orphan boy because now it was dark, and I was lost in swamp country. The searchers lit up turpentine torches and walked along the edges of the swamp, hollering and carrying on, trying to find me. They were frantic, but I could not have been having more fun. I had walked since early the previous morning, and now I was still walking for the second night. I was walking along in the dark, looking at fireflies, gazing at the stars in ways I had never been able to look at them, and listening to sounds. I had never heard barred (hoot) owls, horned owls, and all the wildlife that was carrying on. What an adventure!

It must have been about 8:00 or 9:00 at night when I saw a light coming down the road toward me. I knew the light had to be a car. I was so excited that I was going to get to watch that car go by!

I stopped at the edge of the road and watched the car approach me. The driver stopped right in front of me. It was a car with bubble-gum globes on the top. The man was wearing a big Smokey Bear hat. He rolled the window down. Back then, people had to roll the windows down with a handle. I could hear the window screeching—*Eeee-ee-ee-ee-eeeee*—as he rolled it down. He said to me, "Son, is your name Barry?"

I replied, "How did you know my name?"

The policeman put me in his car and took me back to Myrtle and Henry's' house. I got back in bed and slept through the night in a world of joy. By the time I woke up, Mr. Henry had already gone to work, and Miss Myrtle invited me down for breakfast. Miss Maggie was there, too. We had breakfast, and about an hour later, Mr. Henry came home and walked into the back door. Miss Myrtle said to me, "Barry, Mr. Henry has something he wants to give you."

I walked onto the enclosed back porch. Mr. Henry was standing there, and in his arms, there was an adorable puppy. Mr. Henry dropped down on one knee, and Miss Myrtle dropped down beside him. He said, "Barry, would you be our little boy?"

I immediately said yes, and I never left that home. That's how I was adopted, and it started my love affair with the remarkable Bridger family—and dogs.

Myrtle and Henry Bridger—the most loving, wonderful parents any child could have.
I was blessed to call them Mom and Dad, starting when I was five years old.

Adoption: The Roots of a Virtuous and Honorable Life

Jim

Up to this point in Barry's life, many would say that because he was so young and everything was new, he didn't know how bad off he was as a largely ignored orphan. As I heard Barry talk about his adopted parents, I started to understand why he became such a remarkable man grounded in virtue and honor.

As with most parents, taming Barry's curiosity and refining his character didn't come easy, but they were determined to ensure that Barry would be a shining star for the Bridger family. If only they knew the kind of hero they were raising! Here is Barry's account about his much-improved life, growing up in the Bridger family. His story reveals the factors that shaped him into who he would be in the future.

Barry

After the Bridger family adopted me, I learned how this magnificent, life-changing experience came to be. Here is the backstory.

One afternoon, Miss Myrtle was looking out the window. Across the street, she saw a birthday party in progress at Nettie Van's house. She saw a little boy by himself, leaning against the mimosa tree, with his eyes fixed on her home. That was me.

A few years earlier, Miss Myrtle and Mr. Henry had lost their oldest son, Henry Clyde, who had been studying to be a doctor. During his last year of medical school at the University of North Carolina, he perished from tuberculosis. It broke their hearts.

Miss Myrtle was sitting there that evening, watching the birthday party, and she did not recognize the little boy. She called Nettie Van and asked, "Who is the little boy leaning against the mimosa tree?"

Nettie Van said, "Well, that's the orphan from Durham. The Spake family brought him down. They figured that it made sense for him to come over for Nanette's birthday party."

Miss Myrtle replied, "Well, he keeps looking at our house. I think he wants to come see it."

That's when Nettie Van walked out to the mimosa tree and said to me, "Barry, would you like to go see that house?"

I also found out later that when I went to bed that night, Miss Myrtle turned to Mr. Henry and said, "I want to adopt that boy."

Mr. Henry said, "Are you sure? The Spake family brought him down here, and they're thinking about adopting him."

She replied, "Would you mind if I called the Spake family to ask if they will step aside?"

Mr. Henry said, "Go ahead."

She called Mrs. Spake and said, "If you have no objections, I would love to adopt that little boy, Barry."

I was upstairs in bed by then. Mrs. Spake had replied, "We'll be glad to step aside. He and Ellis don't get along well anyway, so I think this would be best for Barry."

Then Miss Myrtle turned to Mr. Henry and said, "Henry, they have given me permission to adopt that little boy. You need to call Uncle Gyp."

Uncle Gyp was a politician in the state senate of North Carolina; he was also the North Carolina highway commissioner. He was affectionately known as Uncle Gyp because he was a very shrewd politician and businessman.

Mr. Henry called Uncle Gyp and said, "Gyp, Miss Myrtle wants to adopt that orphan boy who came down with the Spake family to visit the Hillburns."

Uncle Gyp said, "Ah, she doesn't want to do that."

Mr. Henry told him, "Yes, she does. Take care of it."

I never left the house. That's how I was adopted. That's the way they did it back in the 1940s. It was amazing.

The next day, they tried to send me to school, and I ran away. They sent me to school for about a week, and I ran off every day. I was still enjoying looking at all that life had to offer, all the things I had never seen.

A rambunctious and happy young boy—my school photo in the first grade.

No Desire to Meet My Birth Mother

When the Bridgers said they wanted to adopt me, I immediately began calling them "Mom" and "Dad." One day twelve years later, when I was about seventeen years old, my mother asked me, "Barry, would you like to have contact with your real mother?"

Without a micron of hesitation, I said, "No. You're my mom."

She later told me that my birth mother was a University of Carolina coed, and my father was an influential businessman from New York. I never asked for additional details. I could not have been more blessed with the mom and dad the Lord gave me. They were incredible people. They taught me virtue, but it took me a long time to realize just how important virtue is. Putting other people ahead of your own personal interests is the path to a fulfilled life.

Falling in Love with the Great Outdoors

I rapidly developed an incredible love of the great outdoors.

When I was six, I begged for a shotgun because my adopted brother, McRae (also known as Mac), a fighter pilot in the South Pacific, was a big-time outdoorsman. He loved to quail-hunt, and he had bird dogs. He was thinking, "Well, if this little orphan wants to go hunting, I'll let him carry the shells." So he put his shell vest around my chest, and it dwarfed me. I walked behind him all day. Boy, I learned to walk because that sucker could walk all day long and hunt. With all that walking, I got very strong, physically.

By the time I hit eight years old, I tried to convince my mom and dad to buy me a shotgun. I told them I'd do anything they asked. I really wanted my own shotgun. So they gave me a .410 shotgun at age eight, and I would hunt with it. I taught my English shepherd dog how to point quail. On opening day of hunting season that year, I went out and killed eight quail. I walked into my house and presented them to my family. My brother came in with his high-powered bird dogs and his buddies about an hour later to eat, and they had only five quail among them. So I was doing OK as a little boy with a 410.

I quickly learned to mimic all types of bird and animal sounds. I would go out and ask the farmers if I could quail-hunt on their property. They'd say, "Well, first of all, you've got to help me with the crow population. They're eating all my peanuts. Would you mind going crow hunting?"

I said, "I can do that right now." I could call crows and was a good shot. Helping the farmers trim the crow flock was a gateway for me to hunt quail on their property.

I also learned to call ducks and other animals with my voice—just about anything that made a noise. I was constantly outside, trying to mimic everything I heard, starting at age six. By the time I

Sailing with my dad, not long after I was adopted.

was ten, I could mimic all the wildlife in our area. Then I got into fishing. Hunting and fishing have been passions of mine ever since.

Early in my life, when I wasn't outdoors, my entertainment came from movie theaters. My favorite actors were Tom Mix, Lash LaRue, Roy Rogers, Gene Autry, Red Rider, and the like. In those days, some of the movie stars came to town and performed on stage. Lash LaRue could pop off a Coke bottle cap while someone held the bottle. Movies were a big deal. All five hundred people in our town would go to the movies. When I was about ten years old, we got our first TV. There was just a sparkle on the screen, and a vague little image would show up. We'd say, "Look. Look there. I think it's a guy." I loved Westerns, particularly *The Rifleman*. However, most of my entertainment came from the outdoors.

When I was eight years old, I hunted bobwhite quail and turtle doves. It was great fun for me to take my dog, Duke, quail or dove hunting. There was plenty of game to hunt, so it was like being in heaven for me. I also loved to hunt ducks. I was able to call them. We called wood ducks "squealers" because of the sound they made. Miss Maggie cooked the ducks I brought home, which was a treat for me.

My brother and I loved to fish. But I never got into fly fishing because I grew up in the swamps. There was so much undergrowth that trying to use a fly rod would be impossible. I usually fished for bass, brim, catfish, and tadpoles.

Always Be Learning (ABL)

Jim

Those who are familiar with me know that I am a lifelong learner. I learned from Barry that there was so much I didn't know because my experiences were different from others. That's true for all of us.

As I reflect on Barry's life, I know him to be a person who is constantly trying to better himself through learning. That's why this section is titled "Always Be Learning"—ABL for short, as the blog post I mentioned earlier refers to it.

Barry is a lifelong learner, too. One of his most memorable learning opportunities came when a stubborn pony named Dan decided to, as the old saying goes, "head for the barn.

Barry
Dan, the Pony

As soon as I knew there was such a thing as a pony, I begged for one. I was eight or nine when the Bridger family gave me a pinto pony. I named him Dan. Pinto ponies have a deserved reputation for being mean tempered. I was to discover that the hard way.

I quickly decided that I wasn't going to ride with a saddle. I was going to ride like the Indians I had seen on TV—bareback. I learned quickly, and boy, could I ride bareback! I rode like a Comanche warrior turning a herd of bison.

One thing to learn about horses—in particular, ponies: when it's time to go to bed and darkness is falling, a pony wants to get that last bit of grub that he is fed every evening at a certain time. The pony knows the food is waiting. If you turn his head toward the barn and it's a mile away, that's 'going to be a short mile in terms of time.

One evening, Dan and I were heading to the barn, trotting along slowly. Off to the right was a paved road. On my left was a row of huge loblolly pine trees. There was a sidewalk between that row of loblolly trees and the paved highway. I made a mistake—I loosened up the reins. That was a signal to Dan to take off, and once he committed, I could not stop him.

I was pulling hard on the reins, but it was no use. I looked up, and in front of me were two local schoolteachers, Mrs. Stone and Mrs. Crowder, walking on the sidewalk with their backs to me. They did not see or hear me coming. Dan was galloping toward those ladies at about thirty miles an hour. I continued to pull on the reins as hard as I could, but Dan had no intention of stopping. As my pony hurtled toward the two ladies, a big transfer truck came rumbling down Main Street toward us. The teachers could not move off the sidewalk because of the loblolly pines on their left and the approaching truck on their right. I screamed to the women at the top of my lungs, "Get out of the way!"

It was too late. Dan slammed into the women, knocking one into the street and the other into a pine tree. Dan never slowed down, all the way to the barn.

Knowing I was in serious trouble, I quickly slipped back into my house after dropping Dan off at the barn. Mrs. Stone and Mrs. Crowder were already there. They looked like they'd been in a fight with a bobcat. They wanted to know why I ran over them. I confessed to running over them, and I apologized profusely. I was so grateful that they were not seriously injured. I thought for sure I had killed Mrs. Crowder. I thought she fell under that truck and was dead. And I couldn't imagine that Mrs. Stone could have bounced any higher off that damn loblolly pine tree than she did!

Later on, I was a student of Mrs. Stone and Mrs. Crowder. They were tough on me but finally came to believe that I didn't hit them on purpose. They finally understood that no matter how hard I tried, the pony would not slow down because he was heading to the barn. Plus, I couldn't stop Dan because I didn't weigh much, and I was riding bareback, with no saddle or stirrups. I wanted to be wild, like an Indian. And, boy, was I!

Lesson from a Pony

One of my favorite pastimes was to show off my bareback riding skills to my friends. A favorite trick was to bridle Dan and face him directly away from me. I would then run toward his rear end, jump high into the air, place my hands on his rump, and land in the saddle as he galloped away.

But one day, as I was showing off for some of my buddies, my trick did not go so well. As I ran toward Dan's rear end, he timed my leap perfectly. As I leaped into the air, he kicked me in the chest. *Thwack!* I dropped to the ground like a sack of pota-toes. As Dan looked back at me, I could almost hear him say, "How'd you like that?"

SEASON'S GREETINGS

My parents used this photo of me on Dan the pony on the Christmas cards they sent out in 1949. He and I were a great match because we were both always looking for some fun to get into.

As you might expect, I never did that trick again. I never trusted him after that. That kick was transformative, life changing.

A Formula for Love: An Orphan and His Adoptive Parents

Jim

Barry learned many things as he pursued his lifetime of learning—how to be a loving parent, the importance of virtues and values, how to be successful in life, and a host of other valuable lessons from the Bridgers. Next, Barry describes the love shared between parents and a child and how love can transform loneliness.

Barry

I experienced much loneliness early in life due to growing up in an orphanage. Something was missing: love. Little did I know that later in life, I would be alone again during the Vietnam War. The loneliness would be different that time because of what happened in the Bridger family.

Mr. Henry and Miss Myrtle Bridger considered me a gift to replace the sadness they felt over the loss of their son. And they were the right combination to help me through my formative years. Their love was unmatched, and they patiently allowed a precocious boy such as me learn how to deal with life's challenges. During those years, I could be quite difficult to deal with due to my incredible energy and hard-headedness. They gave me opportunities to grow and to face the inevitable challenges of life.

My recollections of family life were very positive because of the love I gave to and received from my adoptive parents. I learned many things from my parents: self-discipline, the joy of being part of a family, my incredible faith, and how to be happy in life. I cannot thank my adoptive parents enough for all they gave this little boy who had nothing. I often think about what it would've been like if they had not adopted me and I was left to live in the orphanage, like so many children.

I was extremely fortunate to experience the family life provided by the Bridgers and am happy to be called a Bridger. Mr. Henry and Miss Myrtle were not pushovers when it came to parenting, but they did show me what it was like to grow up surrounded by love. This allowed me to start on the journey of a very happy life, despite my difficult start in an orphanage.

Maggie's Unforgettable Home-Cooked Meals

Although Mum a jug jug i e so swack i nono du d love love sometimes enticed me with cobbler and other delicious home cooking, sometimes it was not easy going when it came to vegetables. I cannot count the times my mother said, "You're going to have to eat your spinach if you want to go watch Roy Rogers at the movies this afternoon."

I hated greens, particularly spinach. I asked her, "How much do I have to eat?"

She showed me, and I would swallow some vinegar to choke down a bit of spinach, swallowing it without chewing it. I inhaled every damn bit of it, and then I got to go see Roy Rogers at the movie theater.

Maggie—Mum a jug jug i e so swack i nono du d love love—cooked collard greens and mustard greens, and those were equally offensive to me. She also cooked quail, pheasant, and duck. She was a great duck cooker. Oh, she could cook it all. I can't tell you what a wonderful thing it was to sit down at the table and have such a delicious meal, along with homemade pie—except for that damn spinach. My mom ate all kinds of vegetables, but not me. I'd much rather have Baby Ruth candy bars.

The Heritage of Bladenboro, North Carolina

My dad was an absolutely brilliant man. He was as nice as he could be, and he espoused every quality you could ever ask for in a human being. He was incredibly smart. He was kind. He was hard working. He spoke little, said much.

For a living, he did about everything you can do. He was a farmer. He also ran the Bridger Corporation, which was a general store. Back in those days, they sold mules, fertilizer, and all kinds of things at the general store. He was a crop insurance salesman. He ran a cotton mill and a peanut mill. He also ran a bank. He was president of the Bladenboro Oil Mill and of the Bladenboro Peanut Mill. The man was in everything you can think of. He had all kinds of land. The Bridger clan in Bladenboro was the predominant family, by a long shot. They were lawyers, doctors, farmers, and businesspeople—people who did well because they worked hard. For the most part, as far as I ever knew, they were honest, caring, and respectful folks. You've got to be proud of people like the Bridgers from the Carolinas. They are a great example of what people were like in my community and should be like today.

My parents had many relatives. The whole town was full of uncles and aunts. Two brothers came to Bladenboro in the 1800s and founded that town. Retired Army Lieutenant General Caslen[3], a former superintendent of the US Military Academy, asked me if I was related to the Bridgers who founded Bladenboro, North Carolina. I told him, "Yes. My great-grandfather was one of the founders, along with his brother."

These two founders of Bladenboro started off in the early 1800s by opening a cotton mill, an oil mill, and a general store. The town expanded from there.

---

3   In July 2019, Army Lieutenant General Robert L. Caslen, Jr., was selected to serve as the twenty-ninth president of the University of South Carolina in Columbia. He is a former superintendent and president of the US Military Academy at West Point. See the USC press release at https://www.sc.edu/uofsc/posts/2019/07/president_elect_caslen.php.

Chapter 3

ADOPT VALUES THAT WILL GUIDE YOUR FUTURE DECISIONS

Jim

Barry's love of learning continued through his formative years. His love of the outdoors, learning, and absorbing those virtues, which he developed from those who loved him, shaped him into a mature young man, although he continued to be precocious. As Barry reflected on his early life, it was clear that he sought much more fulfillment than his life in the orphanage gave him. As he tells this part of the story, you will see how he built habits that started to contribute to his eventual persona.

By the way, in this chapter, Barry describes how he mastered doing one-handed handstands. Later, in chapter 10, you'll read about—and see impressive photos of—how he retaught himself this feat after suffering torture at the hands of his North Vietnamese captors.

Barry

In the fall of the year I was adopted, I entered first grade. I was six years old. The first thing I did when they dropped me off at the schoolhouse was run away. I just wanted to go out and look at the oak trees, those loblolly pines, and all that stuff I'd never seen before. It was such an adventure because everything was so wonderfully different from anything I'd known in life. I kept running away from school to go explore the great outdoors.

I'm still the same way, really. Even now, my wife gets phone calls from time to time from some of our friends in Missouri, where we live. They say to her, "Please don't let Barry go back onto the Missouri River by himself at night."

The Missouri River is the fifth-fastest-flowing river in America, primarily because of all the water being channeled by levees and dikes. It is one of the most treacherous rivers in the world, and the current runs about eight miles per hour. If you ever stand on the riverbank at night, you will not believe how it sounds. You can hear it howling. It's a weird sound. Along its bank is great wild-turkey hunting, and you must be there early in the morning to take advantage of that. So my wife tells my buddies, "You can't stop him. He just goes."

That's just me, and the challenges with the Missouri River continue to this day. Recently, I was fishing on the river when a tremendous storm arose at the same time my engine stopped working. Lightning struck all around me as I sailed down the river with no control. I called Sheila, my wife, and told her I was out of control and to notify the authorities that I needed to be rescued. I spotted a barge that had some large cleats. I took my rope and lassoed a cleat, which brought me to an abrupt halt. The question that Sheila had a hard time explaining to the water authorities was, where I was on the water, since I was on the line between Kansas and Missouri. This shows how I continue to get into trouble when it comes to hunting and fishing. I doubt that it will change

It took a while before the teachers in elementary school could settle this kid down to the point that I'd stay where they put me. To help, they introduced me to a cousin, Joe Bridger, who became my pal and made sure I stayed in school through the eighth grade.

As far as high school in my hometown, I think my parents agreed that the children weren't receiving a serious educational experience, with some exceptions. For example, we were required to take a course in civics. I do believe that course had a profound impact on me because it taught me about the purpose of the rules of law, the basic elements of the Constitution, and the importance of treating people in accordance with laws rather than our personal whims. And the English classes were very good because the ladies teaching English really meant business. But regarding a lot of the basics of math and science, we didn't have the kind of instruction we needed.

I Discovered Sports

When I was in the eighth grade, the teachers started putting us into intramural sports and the like. The basketball coach noticed that I was very aggressive on the basketball court. I did things for my size you wouldn't expect me to do, but it was out of determination and desire. In the orphanage, we had no way to do anything without a fight. We had to struggle to have access to a ball, or a bat, or even to have a favorite spot to stand where nobody would push us off.

I Could Not Understand Segregation

Our high school was completely segregated. There were anywhere from twelve to twenty-five kids in my high school classes, but there were zero black kids. They had their own school system at that time in a part of our town we called Colored Town. In 1954, the Supreme Court decided that "separate but equal" wasn't going to work in the *Brown vs. Board of Education* decision. But segregation did not lose its ugly grip on the South and my community right away at all. It took a while, and I was always conflicted about it.

We'd be working our butts off doing something on the farm, and my buddy would say, "We'll give the black guys some watermelon, but they don't eat with us." That made no sense to me, so I ignored him. It still makes me emotional to think about it.

The way I look at it is that hardworking people are hardworking people, regardless of their background race, religion, etc. Unfortunately, that was not the approach where I came from. I am glad things changed.

How Bob Wood Got Me into Sewanee Military Academy

Eventually, my mother concluded that I wasn't receiving the education I needed to take advantage of my basic skills. So she called McCallie Military Academy High School, where my brother, McRae, had been a student years earlier. McCallie was an excellent prep academy in western North Carolina, near Chattanooga, Tennessee. If they would accept me, cost was not an issue. When my mother called to ask about a place for me for my junior year, they told her I'd have to take a battery of exams to see if I qualified academically.

They sent the battery of tests to my math instructor in Bladenboro, who then administered the tests and sent the results back to McCallie. Unfortunately, they called my mother not long after that to say that I was not academically gifted enough to handle the work at McCallie. This news nearly broke my mother's heart, but I was delighted because that meant I could stay in my hometown and play football during my junior and senior years.

At that time, I still had a self-serving attitude, which prevented me from seeing the big picture.

But that summer, while our family was on vacation, my mother struck up a conversation with a man named Bob Wood, who was sitting near her on the beach. I was on the beach throwing a ball about a hundred feet in the air and running underneath to catch it with one hand. Eventually, my mother asked the man she was talking to where he worked. He revealed that he was a math and physics instructor at Sewanee Military Academy, which was near McCallie Military Academy. They had a lengthy conversation about my not being able to get into McCallie. He told my mother he'd like to meet me, so she invited him over for supper.

When Mr. Wood came over for supper that night, I didn't know who he was, and I didn't know about the conversation he and my mom had on the beach. But after supper, Mom walked into another room, and Mr. Wood said, "Barry, come over to the kitchen table. I want to ask you a couple of questions."

I walked over, and he said, "I want you to add these two fractions for me. How much is one-half and two-thirds?"

I looked at him and replied, "I think you just add the two numbers on the top, which equal three, and the two numbers on the bottom, which equal five, to get the answer of three-fifths."

Mr. Wood explained that I did not understand the rules for adding fractions. He said, "Let me show you something, Barry. Here's the way you do this." He then spent the next two hours instructing me on all kinds of different mathematical rules and concepts. After we covered a concept, Mr. Wood gave me problems to solve. He was measuring my academic prowess. At the end of our conversation, he smiled and asked me to call my mother.

When she entered the room again, he said to her, "Mrs. Bridger, we'd love to have Barry come to Sewanee Military Academy."

So my parents packed me up and sent me to Sewanee for my last two years of high school—a profoundly positive decision that would accelerate my physical, intellectual, and emotional growth and prepare me, like nothing else, to handle the tough times of life.

I had fun at Sewanee Military Academy. I put my head down and embraced everything it had to offer.

Sewanee Military Academy no longer exists, unfortunately.

Sewanee Military Academy No Longer Exists

St. Andrew's-Sewanee School is the result of the 1981 merger of two older institutions, and it builds on the heritage of three Episcopal schools founded on Monteagle Mountain in Franklin County, Tennessee.[4]

The junior department of the University of the South, opened in 1867, went by several different names and enrolled students of various ages but existed longest as the Sewanee Military Academy (SMA).[5]

St. Mary's School for Girls functioned from 1896 to 1968 under the auspices of the Sisters of St. Mary's before the Order ceased its teaching activities. St. Andrew's School,

---

4   Margaret D. Binnicker, "St. Andrew's-Sewanee School," *Tennessee Encyclopedia*, https://tennesseeencyclopedia.net/entries/st-andrews-sewanee-school/.

5   Ibid.

started by Episcopal monks from the Order of the Holy Cross in 1905, began as an elementary school but eventually concentrated on secondary education. Though the schools were quite different in mission in their earlier decades, changes that occurred on the three campuses in the late 1960s led to growing similarities.[6]

When St. Mary's closed, both SMA and St. Andrew's became co-educational. In 1970, the Order of the Holy Cross and its monks withdrew from St. Andrew's and turned the school over to a board of trustees. That same year, the military aspect of SMA was dropped, and its name changed to Sewanee Academy. The evolution of distinctly diverse schools into two campuses attracting the same types of students led to a merger on the St. Andrew's campus immediately adjacent to the domain of the University of the South.[7]

A Natural at Gymnastics

My brother, McRae, was a gifted athlete and a terrific swimmer. He could even walk on his hands really well. I wanted to be just like him, so I worked hard to learn how to do everything he could do. It didn't take long for me to master handstands and walk on my hands.

A few years ago, a news reporter for our local newspaper in Platte City, Missouri, wrote an article about me, and he included a photo of me doing a one-handed handstand.

A Small but Mighty Football Player

When I was in the eighth grade, the teachers started putting us into intramural sports and the like. The basketball coach noticed that I was very aggressive on the basketball court. I did things for my size you wouldn't expect me to do, but it was out of determination and desire. In the orphanage, we had no way to do anything without a fight. We had to struggle to have access to a ball or a bat, or even to have a favorite spot to stand where nobody would push us off.

In my football uniform at Sewanee Military Academy.

---

6   Ibid.
7   Ibid.

In the ninth grade, I got the opportunity to play football. I weighed ninety-three pounds, but I went out for the football team, and I couldn't wait. I played first string. After one of our varsity games, our coach wrote an article about me. He described me this way: "Pound for pound, the toughest kid we have on the squad." That gives you an idea of what a determined little orphan I was and how that orphanage experience really impacted my attitude about life.

Sewanee Military Academy is where I really fell in love with sports, particularly football. I was up to 123 pounds by then, but I always did well for my size. As far as basketball, I wasn't great, but I was good enough to play, and I played a lot. In track, I think my best time for running a mile was five minutes flat. I just never had a lot of speed.

I entered Sewanee Military Academy in my junior year and went out for football. I was an unknown quantity to the coaching staff and my teammates. When I arrived at the first practice, the first-string varsity team was chewing up the practice squad. The second-stringers were clearly terrified. Understandably, the coach was not happy with their performance. He turned to the subs seated on the sidelines and said, "Is there any one among you who wants to play football?"

I jumped to my feet, yelling, "I do!" As I assumed my position at right linebacker, I was greeted with raucous laughter from our opposing 240-lb. first-string varsity center. The sight of my 123 lbs., adorned with unblemished white football pants and jersey, was more than he could stand. With the snap of the ball, I sliced my way between offensive linemen and made the tackle on our fullback, Rip Hawkins, later an All-American football player at the University of North Carolina. The next play was around the right end, with the same results.

Then something very special happened. Every member of the practice squad in the scrimmage and on the sidelines began to spontaneously shout and encourage one another. Their passion for the game returned with a vengeance. It takes only a spark to create a fire. Passion is the fire that gives you the strength to endure the pain to learn, to achieve, to overcome the tough times of life that await us all. After that, our practice squad gave up no quarter to a rival team.

Later that evening, my coach sought me out and asked, "Where did you play football?"

I said, "In North Carolina—a small school, six-man football."

He replied, "You're doing good, kid. I hope you keep up what I saw today."

That was my introduction to Sewanee Military Academy football. My senior year, at 130 lbs., I was voted the most valuable player on the team.

Everybody has the opportunity to take whatever he or she is given and do something with it. I enjoyed doing all kinds of things with my gifts. I had a lot of fun, and still am.

When I started playing sports in high school, I discovered that the same rules applied as in the orphanage. If I was going to make a tackle, I had much to do before I could get to the guy with the ball. I learned that it takes effort, determination, and resilience to make good things happen.

I never met a winner who gave up or a loser who never quit. In the words of author Harriet Beecher Stowe, "Never give up, for that is just the place and time that the tide will turn."

A UNC Tar Heel Who Studied Harder than Anyone

My mom went to Queens University in Charlotte, North Carolina, and majored in music. My father, his brothers, and the rest of the Bridger family, almost to the last person, were big benefactors to Wake Forest University. In fact, some of the buildings on the Wake Forest campus were built with financial gifts from the Bridger family.

That would've been a logical place for me to consider going to college, but I wanted no part of Wake Forest. I was a Tar Heel, and I wanted to go to the University of North Carolina.

My brother was also a student at the University of North Carolina, and he continued to be a big influence on my life and my decisions. My mom and dad, my brothers, and my cousins were all big fans of the UNC Tar Heel football and basketball teams. So it was natural for me to go to UNC after I graduated from Sewanee.

My first recollection of attending a UNC football game was when my brother and his wife, Sarah, took me to a football game between UNC and the University of Tennessee. We lost that game, and I wasn't very happy about it.

Freshmen at the University of North Carolina were required to appear before a board that counseled students on what subjects they could take, what subjects they had to take, and what subjects they didn't need to take. This information was based on the school's assessment of the intellectual savvy of each freshman coming into the school system.

I sat in line for about an hour, waiting to hear about my classes. Then an elderly gentleman called me to his desk. He looked at me, and his first question was, "Where did you go to high school?"

I said, "Sewanee Military Academy."

He said, "Really? Then you won't have any problems. Go over there and sign up for your classes."

That was confirmation that my mom did send me to a great academic institution for my high-school years. The first thing I did after that meeting was to sign up to be in the ROTC (Reserve Officer Training Corps) program. This program was the precursor for my eventual transition into the United States Air Force.

Math: The Answers Are Either Right or Wrong

From the beginning of my college studies, I decided I would try to major in mathematics because in mathematics, the answers to the tests you take and the challenges you must overcome will be either right or wrong. You don't have to write a narrative three pages long to answer a question. In math, there is a specific answer. All you must do is figure out how to get it. I liked that idea.

I'm sure I'm not the only person who thinks this way, but I was sure I was absolutely going to die before I flunked out of the University of North Carolina. One-fourth of the freshmen were gone in the first six months. The school was quite serious about giving hard tests and expecting students to study hard. And because math is either right or wrong, it can get to you quick and hard.

I worked my butt off. I worked at least eight hours a day, every day, studying. The only time I ever allowed myself the privilege of going out and doing anything else was when I went hunting. On Saturday mornings, at the crack of day, until about early afternoon, I allowed myself to go hunting. Then I'd go back to my dorm room and get back to studying.

I shared a room with two roommates, and both were gone in the first six months. They were very smart guys, but they didn't work hard, and it caught up with them. They taught me that I was right about that hard work. You need to stay after it.

I had one huge dilemma at the University of North Carolina: I was so busy studying that I had no time for anything else, including dating. I'd be at the library every night at about 5:00 p.m., and I would get back to my room when it closed every night. I studied every weekend, except for Saturday mornings, when I got in four hours of precious walking in the woods with my shotgun, looking for something like a covey of quail. It was flat-out work.

I had no dates in high school. I had no dates as a freshman or sophomore at Carolina. One day, a buddy of mine who knew I was trying to get a date said to me, "Have you gotten a date yet?"

When I said no, he asked, "Bridger, what the he** are you doing?"

I said, "I don't know. I ask, and they say no."

He replied, "Wait a minute. You're a math major, right?"

I nodded yes, and he said, "You remember that course we took together on permutations and combinations of numbers?"

"Yeah."

"Well, Bridger, come on! It's all about probability. Why don't you ask ten?"

So, I did. I immediately got a hit. I called it the "dating rule of ten."

The moral of that story is this: just because you can do math doesn't mean you're smart.

I Wanted No Part of Fraternity Life

When my brother, McRae, attended UNC, he was in a fraternity. Soon after I arrived at UNC, it was Rush Week. I got invitations to attend parties from every fraternity on the campus. I'm quite confident that part of the reason for that is that my brother worked behind the scenes, encouraging the fraternities, particularly the one he was a member of, to invite me to join a fraternity.

My roommates were saying, "Dang. You got invited to every freaking fraternity on the campus. What are you going to do?"

I said, "I guess I'll go to a couple of them. My brother wants me to go to his fraternity, and I might go to one other." I don't know which fraternity my brother was in, which shows you how little I cared about fraternity life.

But here's what happened: I went to the frat house at about 5:00 p.m., hours before the party began. I thought I'd drop by and just look at the fraternity. I walked in and went downstairs to the party room. They had drawn huge, colorful murals all over the walls of boys and girls doing things that you would only expect to find in a porn movie.

I looked at that and said to myself, "I will not be a part of this fraternity. Why would they do this?" I walked out of there and never went back. To me, it was insulting what they had done. My moral fiber said, "Absolutely not."

Another thing that upset me about fraternities was that too many students at some frat houses seemed to be drinking excessively. In fairness to those whom I thought drank excessively, my attitude was strongly influenced by the fact that I didn't drink at all. I wondered, "How are you going to get the best out of yourselves, bumping into each other and falling on the floor?" A drunken frat party wasn't a place I wanted to be. I had other things to do.

I never had a sip of alcohol the entire time I was at the university. I never had a drink as a fighter pilot, either, and good grief, they drink their share. I drank only water and Cokes. In fact, the first time I ever had a drink of alcohol was when I was thirty-three years old.

Now, I don't mean to suggest I'm a prude because I am not. I know there are fraternities I would have been proud to join. The timing for me just wasn't good. I was not one of the crowd. I marched to a different drummer with different priorities. But that independent spirit helped me overcome difficult trials later in my life.

Chapter 4

STAND ON THE SHOULDERS OF THOSE WHO CAME BEFORE YOU

Jim

We all stand on the shoulders of those who came before us. And, as we live our lives with virtue and integrity, eventually, others will stand on our shoulders to lead the way into the future.

In this chapter, Barry shares how his relationship with his older brother inspired him to become a US Air Force pilot and led him to enjoy the journey of his life.

Who in your life has gone before you, paving the way for you to succeed in life?

Barry

The influence that my brother, McRae, had on me was profound. About the same time he returned from the war zone in the South Pacific, I was a five-year-old kid his parents had just adopted.

McRae left the US Army Air Corps and went to work for our father, who, as I mentioned earlier, was a consummate entrepreneur. At that time, our father was involved in the cotton-ginning business and the oil-mill business; he crushed cottonseed to make oil. That's called a cotton mill. He also ran a peanut mill, a general store, an insurance business, and a bank. He was an incredibly smart individual.

McRae married Ms. Sarah, who was a beautiful lady and smart as a whip. She should've been a contestant in the Miss America contest. During the writing of this book, sadly, Sarah passed away. She was ninety-six years old.

I love this photo of me, sitting atop my brother, McRae's, shoulders on the beach, in 1952. He's just walking along the beach. I'm not holding onto him, and he's not holding onto me. I'm just balancing on his shoulders as he walks. It's as if we're one guy who's eleven feet tall. We did that kind of stuff all the time. I was, literally, standing on the shoulders of the one who came before me.

As I mentioned earlier, in my hometown of Bladenboro, we had two streets that ran parallel to each other: Front Street and Back Street. Tricky to remember. McRae lived on Back Street in a small home after he came home from World War II.

McRae, a Legendary Storyteller

I was immediately attracted to McRae because he was blessed with the capacity to tell great stories. I spent hours at his house in the evenings, if I didn't have homework or if it was on the weekend. Frequently, my cousin, Joe, was with me to listen to McRae tell stories.

One night, McRae was telling a story about the Wild Man of Lake Waccamaw, who had one arm and lived in the woods. Lake Waccamaw is in North Carolina. I still do not know if this story is true. But it was a pretty scary.

After the story was over, it must've been about 9:00 p.m. Joe and I were still scared from that story as we walked back to our homes. My home was in one direction not far from McRae's, and Joe's was in opposite direction. When Joe got home, the house was empty. He was scared after hearing McRae's story, so he crawled under his bed and fell asleep. At about 10:00 that night, my dad got a call from Joe's dad, asking if he knew where Joe was. My dad didn't know.

Joe's parents called the cops, who went out to look for him, riding up and down the street. They finally found Joe, fast asleep under his bed.

An Avid Outdoorsman

Very rapidly after that, I was McRae's shadow. I went everywhere he went. It didn't matter what he was doing, I was always with McRae. He became the gateway to what would become one of the greatest loves of my life—the great outdoors. I can't tell you what a profound impact the great outdoors had on me, in terms of hunting and fishing. It still does today.

McRae was an avid outdoorsman—he hunted and fished. He primarily hunted bobwhite quail with bird dogs. He used English pointers and setters, which were two of the best breeds to hunt quail. Back in those days, there were a lot of quail. That's not true today. They're almost extinct compared to how plentiful they used to be.

Quail season started about the first of November and ended about the first of January. McRae hardly missed a weekend hunting quail. I was right by his side, a teeny boy carrying a vest filled with shotgun shells. It was work to keep up with him because he walked at a rapid pace. That's how I learned to walk fast and get stronger.

McRae also loved fishing. If it wasn't hunting season, McRae was fishing freshwater, or on the ocean. We had a beach cottage at Wrightsville Beach, North Carolina, and we had an ocean-going fishing boat. This allowed McRae, who was also a big-ocean fisherman, to fish for mackerel, king mackerel, bonitos, bluefish, cobias, wahoo, and so forth—even some mahi mahi, better known as a bull dolphin. I was almost always on the boat when McRae went fishing.

He did a lot of freshwater fishing, too, primarily for redbreast sunfish and copperhead bream. The redbreast is a beautiful fish and shaped like a perch. In the swamps of North Carolina, there are a lot of redbreast and copperhead bream.

McRae absolutely loved to get in a boat on the Black River, which is a tributary of the Cape Fear River in southeastern North Carolina. It's about fifty miles long and empties into the ocean at Wilmington, North Carolina. It was less than an hour's drive from our house. There was great fishing in the headwaters of the Black River—perch, brim, and redbreast. McRae absolutely loved to fish that river. Back then, we used catalpa worms, which most people haven't heard of. They live on catalpa trees and are one of the best baits you can use for perch and redbreast.

Always Pulling Pranks

Well, guess who did all the boat paddling? Me.

The Black River has a strong current, three to four miles an hour. McRae would launch the boat. I'd get in the back with a paddle, and McRae sitting up front, happy as a lark, would let me do all the work with my paddle.

I'd say, "Well, let's go."

McRae used to pull tricks on me all the time.

While we were on the river, he'd turn around and look at me in the back of the boat and say, "Barry, I've been fishing on this river for thirty-five years. I've never seen anybody who can paddle a boat like you. Would you like to fish?"

I'd respond, "No, sir! I'm going to paddle this boat."

He would set me up by praising me and then asking me if I wanted to do something I didn't love to do. His strategy worked. I'd say, enthusiastically, "No, no, I want to paddle!"

The Day We Came Face-to-Face with a Cottonmouth Moccasin

The Black River in eastern North Carolina is loaded with cottonmouth moccasins. In the dead of summer, I'm confident you could fill a big lard can with cottonmouths every four miles.

One day, McRae and I were fishing down the river with the current. He was flipping a cork with a catalpa worm. I was sitting in the back of the boat, and I had to back-paddle so we wouldn't go down the river too fast. That river was full of snakes. McRae tilted his head downward because a big tree limb was right in front of him, coming off the riverbank.

As he slid under the limb, he didn't realize it, but a big cottonmouth moccasin was lying on top of that limb. McRae put his head right underneath the cottonmouth moccasin's belly and slid underneath him. That woke up the cottonmouth. That snake rose up off the limb, and now he was looking at me because I was at the back of the boat, sliding toward him. I dug in with the paddle and started back-paddling to stop the boat because I didn't want to go underneath that limb. McRae didn't know what was going on. He turned and said, "Barry, why are you stopping the boat?"

Then he looked that cottonmouth right in the eye. The snake was looking at both of us, wondering which one he was going to get to eat. McRae yelled, "Gosh dang snake!"

He grabbed the paddle he had in the front of the boat and started paddling as hard as he could to drag that boat down the river so he wouldn't get eaten by that moccasin. Well, he was dragging me right toward the moccasin, so I back-paddled like heck to back the boat up.

I had gotten strong because I'd been doing all that paddling. McRae was throwing water every which way, trying to go down the river, and he had the current on his side. But it wasn't doing him any damn good because I was slowly but surely dragging him to a meeting with that cottonmouth. Lucky for my brother, our paddle war caused the boat to move toward the middle of the river, away from the limb and the snake. We were safe. If I had a movie of that, it would be a hit on YouTube.

We had many kinds of adventures such as these while hunting and fishing. This contributed to our brotherly love and closeness while growing up.

My Inspiration to Become an US Air Force Pilot

McRae was in the Ferry Command in the Second World War. He flew all the different aircraft types that were supporting the South Pacific Theater of combat. As I mentioned, he flew the P-51 Mustang, the P-47 Thunderbolt, and the Lockheed P-38. He was an incredible aviator and, in my eyes, the quintessential aviation hero. He was in the old Army Air Corps, which was the precursor for today's United States Air Force.

When he arrived home, he went to work with my father in his myriad of businesses. Back in those days, instead of tractors, we had mules. It would take us almost three weeks to plow a forty-acre field behind a mule. I know—I did it. By the way, today you can plow that forty-acre field in about thirty minutes with the equipment we have now.

McRae used to take me out to the small, local airport in Bladenboro to fly in a Piper PA-18 Super Cub—a two-seat, single-engine monoplane. We flew above the swamps and rivers, which was a treat for a young person. That was a major factor in fanning my appetite to become a fighter pilot. I always wanted to get into the US Air Force and fly the F-104 Starfighter, which was the hot aircraft of its day. It was a single-engine, supersonic interceptor aircraft that later became widely used as an attack aircraft.

By the time I arrived at Webb Air Force Base near Big Spring, Texas, for pilot training, the F-104 Starfighters were all in mothballs. The hottest USAF fighter was now the F-4 Phantom, which was a much more powerful and capable aircraft than the F-104 ever thought of being. The F-4 Phantom was a tandem two-seat, twin-engine, all-weather, long-range supersonic jet interceptor and fighter-bomber that first entered service in 1958 with the US Navy. Even though I didn't get to fly the 104, I was assigned to fly the premier fighter aircraft for the US Air Force, the F-4. After I finished flight training at Webb Air Force Base, I was assigned to MacDill Air Force Base in Tampa, Florida, where I began my career as a USAF fighter pilot.

Training as a jet pilot, I had no idea about the fate that awaited me.

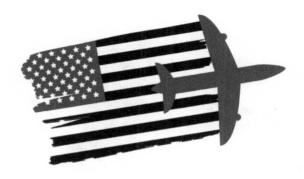

Chapter 5

HOPE FOR THE BEST, BUT PREPARE FOR THE WORST

Jim

Where we end up in life is the result of our series of choices. Barry triumphed in life by taking the road less traveled and selecting the more difficult options available to him. It formed his character, and he navigated those experiences in a fearless manner. That continues to this day. Here is how he ended up as a fighter pilot and what happened on his 75th mission.

Barry

When I was in the ROTC program at the University of North Carolina, I applied to go to pilot training. In my group of seniors in that program, we had four or five people who applied to go to pilot training. Some of those who applied could not pass the physical.

If someone had any medical or sight issues, such as astigmatism, or less than 20/20 vision, the USAF would not accept them for flight school. It was difficult to get into pilot training unless you had perfect health. I did, so off I went to pilot training at Big Spring, Texas, in the class of 64G. I graduated from pilot training in the spring of 1964, during the Vietnam War.

There were about twenty-five men in my pilot training class, but only about twelve graduated. The final group had to declare their aircraft preference for their follow-on assignment. Senior military personnel set up a selection board that made the final decision. We each stated what our preference was. The guys would say, "I want to fly bombers" or "I want to fly a transport-type aircraft" or "I want to be a pilot training instructor" or "I want to become a fighter pilot." We left the room, and the board took our requests into consideration. They made their decisions and informed us where they were going to send us.

I wanted to become a pilot training instructor because I knew I could build up flying time fast. But the board declined my request and told me, "You're going to be a fighter pilot." They sent me to MacDill Air Force base to be trained in the F-4 Phantom as a US Air Force fighter pilot.

Only Night Missions—Except for My One Ill-Fated Daytime Mission

The F-4 Phantom was a tandem-seat aircraft, one seat behind the other. The USAF elected to crew the aircraft with two pilots.

I started off like all the F-4 pilots, as a back-seater, flying as a copilot. We called the person in the backseat of the F-4 Phantom a "GIB" (pronounced "gibb"), which stands for "guy in the back." I flew for about a year as a GIB and headed off to my first assignment overseas, in the Philippine Islands. When I came back, I was upgraded to the front seat of the F-4 as a first lieutenant. Now I was the pilot in command, and my GIB was in the back. I was assigned to Ubon, Thailand, to fly in the 497th Tactical Fighter Squad (TFS), which flew all missions at night. So I was a night fighter pilot.

Two aircraft went together on a mission at night. One was called the flare ship, and the other was the gunner. I was the gunner, which meant I carried the Cluster Bomb Units (CBUs) and rocket munitions, while the flare ship dropped flares. We flew from Ubon, Thailand, all the way to the Gulf of Tonkin, a body of water located off the east coast of North Vietnam. Then we lowered our aircraft down until we broke out of the clouds. There was almost always a lot of weather along the coast of North Vietnam.

When we broke out of the clouds, we had to have at least 500 feet of altitude ground clearance to operate. Weather permitting, we turned inbound toward the land. While the flare ship dropped flares, the gunner aircraft looked for trucks that were going down Highway 1. Our mission was to interdict truck traffic, which was supplying the North Vietnamese and the Viet Cong forces. Highway 1 was the only viable north-south road to handle truck traffic. The Vietnamese trucked supplies out of Hanoi, which was about one hundred miles to the north. The Vietnamese took these supplies down Highway 1 and crossed through the demilitarized zone (DMZ) into South Vietnam.

That's what I did until that fateful day I was allowed to fly my first and only daytime mission. Like every other fighter pilot, I wanted to shoot down a MiG. Unfortunately, it was during that mission that I was shot down.

Before a fighter pilot could come home after assignment to the Vietnam combat theatre, he had to fly one hundred missions. If he completed one hundred missions, the Air Force sent him home. The pilot's tour of duty was over for at least another year or so. I was on my seventy-fifth mission when I was shot down. Statistically, you had a 25 percent chance of not completing one hundred missions. Every twenty-five pilots out of one hundred got shot down, killed, or whatever. You had a 75 percent chance of making it back, but there was a 25 percent chance that you wouldn't.

One of the advantages of nighttime flying was that the enemy couldn't see you to shoot at you. Their radar systems were not that good. We also flew so low that it didn't help them much. I arrived in the combat theatre in September, and I was shot down in January. Nighttime missions were very demanding. You had to know what the heck you were doing, or you'd run into a mountain and kill yourself. We flew almost all those missions with at least three-quarters of moonlight. If we didn't have moonlight, and if we didn't have clouds that were high enough so that we could operate underneath them, then we would abort the mission.

Daylight missions were almost exclusively carried out against strategic targets such as airfields, oil depots, bridges, and railheads. These targets were clustered almost exclusively around the capital city of Hanoi in north central Vietnam and the port city of Haiphong in northeast Vietnam. These strategic targets were heavily defended by a colossal assemblage of anti-aircraft weapons and SA-2 missile SAM sites. In other words, the greatest threat to being shot down was attacking targets in and around the cities of Hanoi and Haiphong in northern North Vietnam. My mission was much safer than nighttime interdiction in southern North Vietnam. The proof: I flew one daylight mission in the Hanoi area, and then I was sitting in the Hanoi Hilton prison.

My Commanding Officer: Robin Olds, a Colorful Figure

We were staging the bulk of our air combat operations to attack North Vietnam out of Ubon, Udorn, and Takli Airfields in Thailand. Colonel Robin Olds was the Commanding Officer of the 8th Tactical Fighter Wing, to which I was assigned. At the end of the Vietnam War, he was assigned to the United States Air Force Academy as the Commandant of cadets. He was a colorful figure, a triple ace, a fighter pilot's fighter pilot—one of a kind. He retired in 1973 as a Brigadier General and is now deceased.

About General Robin Olds

General Olds is rated a triple ace, having shot down a total of 17 enemy aircraft during World War II and the Vietnam War. He began his combat flying in a P-38 Lightning named "Scat 1" during World War II, and at the end of the war he was flying Scat VII, a P-51 Mustang. Olds was eventually credited with 107 combat missions and 24.5 victories, 13 aircraft shot down, and 11.5 aircraft destroyed on the ground.[8]

During the Vietnam War in October 1966, Olds entered combat flying in Southeast Asia in "Scat XXVII," an F-4 Phantom II. He completed 152 combat missions, including 105 over North Vietnam. Using air-to-air missiles, he shot down two MiG-17 and two MiG-21 aircraft over North Vietnam, two of them on one mission. He retired from the US Air Force in 1973.

---

8   "Olds, Robin," The National Aviation Hall of Fame, https://www.nationalaviation.org/our-enshrinees/olds-robin/.

In 2001, he was enshrined as a member of The National Aviation Hall of Fame. He died in 2007 at the age of eighty-four.[9]

As an act of defiance toward a US military that was providing him with poorly trained pilots and lackluster support during the Vietnam War, Robin Olds grew a large handlebar mustache, which was a direct violation of Air Force grooming regulations. During the war, most of his superiors found the mustache humorous, but when Olds returned to the United States, he quickly found that not everybody was laughing.[10]

"I remember my first interview with (Air Force Chief of Staff Gen. John P.) McConnell," Olds said. "I walked briskly through the door, stopped, and snapped a salute. He walked up to me, stuck a finger under my nose, and said, 'Take it off!' And I said, 'Yes, sir!' And that was the end of that."[11]

Olds was a fighter pilot's fighter pilot. The senior leadership in the Air Force was scared to death of him because he was the Donald Trump of fighter pilots—you didn't know what he was going to do next. They sent him to the Air Force Academy to try to get rid of him, to get him out of their hair. Robin was known for heavy drinking and was arrested for driving under the influence during these days which probably hurt his future career. He was tough and took chances. Today activity such as heavy drinking is frowned upon, but that was Robin Olds.

US Air Force Survival Training

Survival training that all US Air Force personnel received before they went into a war zone focused on two things:

1. Survival in the jungle or in any harsh environment in which you were trying to escape and evade
2. Surviving as a prisoner of war

They simulated those two situations as best they could. They gave us tough practice interrogations.

---

9   Ibid.
10 Ibid.
11 Ibid.

During our training, we were placed in small boxes to see how we reacted to being confined to a small space. If you had a claustrophobic reaction, you probably would not be sent to the war zone because the trainers were quite confident you'd have to deal with similar conditions in an actual POW camp. When they put me in a box, I had an initial claustrophobic response that caused me to involuntarily flex my shoulder muscles. The boards of my box immediately begin to crack and splinter. I immediately settled down because I realized I could break out of my confinement at will.

Chapter 6

GAIN WISDOM FROM FAILURE

Jim

We learn best by failing as we set out to achieve the goals we have in life. Most of us prefer to have things turn out as anticipated—but often, something goes wrong, and life is disrupted. When Barry's 75th mission as a pilot during the Vietnam War ended in a horrific way, he approached this difficult situation with the same tenacity he demonstrated when facing other life obstacles.

Barry

The Soviet MiG-21s were constantly attacking our fighter-bomber aircraft that were bombing strategic targets in the Hanoi area. The majority of USAF fighter-bomber missions were flown by the F-105 Thunder Chief and the F-4 Phantom. The F-105 Thunder chief is primarily an air-to-ground fighter-bomber, whereas the F-4 Phantom is primarily an air-to-air fighter.

Daily, our fighter-bombers would depart airfields in Thailand and enter Hanoi airspace from the northwest to attack strategic targets such as airfields, railheads, and petroleum depots—all kinds of infrastructure in the Hanoi area. The MiG-21s were gunning primarily for the F-105s, which were totally dedicated to dropping bombs on critical North Vietnamese infrastructure.

We were losing lots of aircraft. Operation Bolo was our opportunity to get even.

About Colonel Robin Olds's Victorious OPERATION BOLO

Led by Col. Robin Olds, OPERATION BOLO used a brilliant deception tactic that destroyed half of the North Vietnamese MiG-21 fighter force, with no USAF losses.[12]

In late 1966, the USAF was not permitted to bomb North Vietnamese airfields and could only destroy enemy fighters in the air. Complicating the problem, enemy MiGs focused on bomb-laden F-105s and only initiated combat when they had a clear advantage. Col. Robin Olds, 8th Tactical Fighter Wing (TFW) commander, and the wing's tactics officer, Capt. John "J. B." Stone, devised a masterful plan to lure and trap North Vietnamese MiG-21s by mimicking an F-105 bombing formation.[13]

On January 2, 1967, 8th TFW F-4s entered North Vietnam from the west using the same route, altitude, and formation as an F-105 bomb strike. They also carried and operated electronic jamming pods used by F-105s. The North Vietnamese took the bait, and the MiGs came up to intercept what they thought was an F-105 strike. At the same time, 366th TFW F-4s came into North Vietnam from the east to block the MiGs' escape to China and to orbit their bases, preventing the MIG's from landing.[14]

Despite problems caused by overcast weather, OPERATION BOLO was triumphantly successful. During the twelve-minute engagement, seven North Vietnamese MIG-21s—about half their operational force—were shot down with no USAF losses. Four days later, another ruse, this time mimicking an F-4 reconnaissance flight, shot down two more MiG-21s. These crippling losses greatly reduced MIG activity for several months.[15]

---

12   "OPERATION BOLO," May 18, 2015, National Museum of the US Air Force™, https://www.nationalmuseum.af.mil/Visit/Museum-Exhibits/Fact-Sheets/Display/Article/196006/operation-bolo/.

13   Ibid.

14   Ibid.

15   Ibid.

Setting a Trap for the North Vietnamese: The BOLO 2 Mission

About a month after the BOLO mission, Olds said, "I'll bet you those people up there in Hanoi have forgotten about Operation Bolo. Why don't we pretend we're 105s again?" I couldn't have been happier to be selected for that mission because I might have a chance at a MiG.

Before we took off, we were briefed on a new electronic pod (QR 160) we would be carrying that would protect our aircraft from SAM missiles by jamming the guidance signal between the Fan Song radar and the SA-2 missiles that the North Vietnamese were using to shoot down our aircraft. We were also briefed to fly in a tight formation when carrying the QRC 160 pod, to maximize its effectiveness, and to not take evasive action, but let the pod protect the flight.

It was also emphasized that, "If your pod does not work, fly up close to an aircraft in your flight with a functioning pod, and it will protect both aircraft."

Six and a half years later, when I came out of Hanoi and returned to flying, we received a different briefing. It said, "Flying in pod formation requires all flight members to fly with an operational QRC 160 pod. If your pod does not work, do not fly up next to an aircraft in your flight. You will double the reflected radar energy, be detected, and shot down." In other words, the correct advice was quite different. There I was, flying up close to my element leader to let his pod jam for both of us, since my pod was not working, not knowing that I was doing precisely the wrong thing. I did take evasive action, but too late.

If you can't take a joke, don't become a fighter pilot.

That was BOLO 2, and the day my copilot and I were shot down—January 23, 1967.

My F-4 Phantom Is Destroyed by a North Vietnamese Missile

The day I was shot down, I had an operational RAW scope, which was a piece of electronic gear that could detect any air defense system that was emitting a radar signal that was hitting my aircraft. An operational QRC 160 pod precluded the simultaneous use of the raw scope. My QRC 160 pod was inoperable, so I was able to use my RAW scope to monitor and alert our flight leader to all potential radar-based air defense threats impacting our mission.

I got a radar signal from left 10:00 o'clock and left 8:00 o'clock. They were Fan Song acquisition radars signals, not missile guidance radar signals. I knew the difference. I could see everything that was looking at us from the ground.

I told part of the story about being shot down over Hanoi in chapter 1. Here is the rest of the story.

My copilot, Capt. Dave Grey, was a very nice guy, a big guy about six foot two, probably 180 or 190 pounds. He was severely injured when he ejected. The F-4 Phantom, back in that day, had a cartridge ejection system. To eject you from the aircraft, it would fire a cartridge, just like shooting a shotgun shell. The cartridge system would hit you in the butt with an enormous amount of force. About 75 percent of the people who were ejected from the F-4 Phantom using the old cartridge system had severe back issues later in life. Dave and I were no exception.[16]

Dave was hurt so severely when he ejected using the cartridge system that one of the vertebrae in his back looked like it was flying on the right side of his spinal column. After that, he could never again fly an ejection-seat aircraft. Another ejection might have seriously injured him or even killed him. Once he got back home, they put him in T-39s, which are non-ejection-seat aircraft.

I saw Dave fall through a deck of clouds. He hit the ground long before me because he was a much bigger guy. He fell faster. By the time I came out of the cloud deck, he'd already been captured. I landed almost in the Hỏa Lò prison camp in downtown Hanoi, so I had nowhere to go.

Years later, when we returned home, Dave told me that just as I rolled upside down and we were going straight down through the clouds, he saw a missile about the size of a telephone pole coming into the backseat of our aircraft. The explosion blew the right wing, half of the left wing, and the tail off

---

16   *Author's note:* Barry says that six years after he got out of Hanoi, the US Air Force changed the ejection mechanism to a rocket boost rather than a cartridge system. With that system, Barry says that when you eject from an aircraft, a rocket boost starts you off slow and then increases the pressure, so you don't get slammed in the rear end with maximum force instantaneously.

our aircraft. Of course I heard the explosion, but I didn't know exactly what had happened to the aircraft.

Dave is OK. He's able to get along as well as would be expected, but he does carry that injury in his back.

Thank God for the Nylon Swim Trunks I Had Tucked into My Flight Suit

The cloud deck above the ground was probably 500 to 1,000 feet; the clouds were heavy and dense that day. I drifted out of that last deck of clouds right over downtown Hanoi. Immediately, Vietnamese military personnel started shooting at me with rifles. I could hear the bullets whizzing by my body—*zip, zip, zip, zip*. I came into view quickly, so they didn't have time to focus and shoot accurately. Thank God I didn't get hit.

As soon as I landed on the ground, people who had what appeared to be very hostile intent surrounded me. Some of them were militia, or military people, and others were peasants who had armed themselves with sticks.

I got to my feet, and I was bleeding profusely from my head wound. The first thing they wanted to do was blindfold me. One of the things I had done in preparation for a possible shoot-down was to put my black nylon swim trunks in my flight suit. I figured that if I was ever shot down and landed in an environment where I could maneuver, I might have to do some swimming across canals or rivers. If that happened, I needed a bathing suit to protect my other clothing so I wouldn't be constantly cold.

As the Vietnamese were trying to figure out how to blindfold me, I pointed to a pocket zipper on my flight suit. They opened it up and found my swim trunks. I don't think they knew what the black thing was, but they were elated that they had found something that would make a great blindfold. They pulled the black nylon swimsuit over my head, thinking my vision would be totally blanked out, because it was black. What they didn't realize is that I could see right through the nylon.

These folks were upset with me for arriving in their country without their permission. They wanted to play games with me and take some vengeance on an American pilot. So they put that swimsuit over my head, tied my hands behind my back with wire, and ran me through a ditch, as fast as they could run, trying to make me trip. I am a lot bigger than the Vietnamese men and women. I pretended that I was about to trip, but I never quite did because I could see. That saved me a lot of potential additional wounds and injuries, just by having that little bathing suit in my flight suit.

After they played their game and were exhausted, a Jeep showed up with the local military commander. They put me in the Jeep. Immediately, a female Vietnamese military member pushed me forward in the Jeep and saw that my wrists were tied behind my back with wire. She removed the wire and put a rope bond on my wrists instead. That was a humanitarian act, an example of being reasonable. I appreciated her attitude.

After a while, they pulled me out of the Jeep and sat me on an anthill. They were grabbing ants and throwing them on me. I sat there, not moving. I didn't want to give the ants a reason to think I was alive. Whenever they threw an ant on me, I could turn a little bit and make the ant land where I wanted it to instead of on my head, for example. I did it in a subtle way so they wouldn't realize I was really seeing the whole show through my nylon bathing suit.

Then my copilot, Dave, showed up. They put him in the Jeep. Dave had a real blindfold on, so he couldn't see. Then they carted us to the Hanoi Hilton.

A News Article About the Day I Was Shot Down

The following details about the day I was shot down appeared on the POW Network website:[17]

On January 23, 1967, Capt. Barry Bridger and his copilot were flying on a mission over North Vietnam when their F-4 Phantom Jet was hit by a surface-to-air missile. The plane burst into flames and fell beneath the cloud layers. No parachutes were seen, nor were beeper signals heard, so Barry was carried in a "missing in action" status. In

---

17 "Bridger, Barry Burton," POW Network, https://www.pownetwork.org/bios/b/b098.htm. [*Note:* They spelled Barry's middle name incorrectly on this site; it should be Bruton, not Burton.]

early 1970, Hanoi acknowledged his presence there. Barry's family received their first letter from him in May 1970.

The following is an excerpt from the book *We Came Home*, written by Barbara Powers Hyatt and published in 1977:[18]

Barry is five feet, nine inches tall and weighs 150 pounds. He has dark hair, green eyes, and a fair complexion. The strong jawline and penetrating eyes speak of the strength and determination of his personality, the broad shoulders and muscular physique indicate the athlete who neither smoked nor drank. His interests are many, but the greatest before his internment were hunting, fishing, dog training (especially Labradors), guitar playing, automobiles, motorcycles, and girls. There is a serious side, too, a faith in God instilled in him by his loving parents.

From the time of landing in the midst of seventy-five people, during the ride to Hanoi and during his first interrogation session, he could feel that it might be a long ordeal and days might be quite grim. Immediately he was put in straps with manacles around his wrists. An eight-foot strap was then woven between and around his arms from the wrists to the shoulders, pulling his arms together until his shoulders came out of their sockets. He suffered through seven excruciating days of straps, ropes, beatings, and handcuffs with no food, sleep or water—he finally printed with his left hand (he is right-handed) a bogus mission statement and not the apology to the Vietnamese people that he was supposed to write and sign "They finally get you and then you write an innocuous statement, one with as little meaning as possible."

Beatings were at the whim of the guards. They might choose an asinine reason, such as getting up one night or walking across your room, to put you through hours of misery. During his initial interroga-

---

18   Barbara Powers Wyatt, *We Came Home* (POW Publications, 1977), https://www.amazon.com/Came-Hardcover-Barbara-Powers-Wyatt/dp/B000TYRT88/ref=sr_1_2?s=books&ie=UTF8&qid=1543807111&sr=1-2&keywords=We+Came+Home.

tion Barry was repeatedly beaten about. There were two severe head injuries he incurred when he was shot down; they were ignored for seven days of inhuman treatment and then required twenty stitches to close the wounds.

During the long years of captivity, Barry developed a skill in gymnastics. In a seven-by-eight-foot room shared sometimes with other men, Barry practiced his gymnastic maneuvers under the most adverse conditions. In the summer, the room was often like an oven, frequently dark with only a dim light dripping through the cracks of the boarded window. For two reasons, Barry turned to gymnastics: it became apparent that to survive, he would have to remain physically and mentally fit, and secondly to fight boredom. By the time of his release, he had accomplished some great maneuvers—a one-hand handstand on either the right or left hand and fifty handstand push-ups. He even taught himself to juggle. While his hands were manacled together for two months, he found that one way to get control over his hands and wrists was to juggle. He accomplished this feat in a dark cell.

During the final days of his captivity, he taught gymnastics to his fellow prisoners. Brotherhood was a basic principle among the POWs, said Bridger, and often they carried it to extremes in their efforts to help one another. Each tried to stay in the torture chambers if he could so that others might escape punishment. "We kept hoping the current program would fizzle before they had gone halfway across the camp. It usually did. The North Vietnamese have a hard time carrying out a plan without getting side-tracked."

"The Vietnamese are fanatics about communism," Bridger explained. He gave insights into their actions and statements: "To them, truth is that which serves the revolution. And they regard life very cheaply. Take my first interrogation, for example. They said, 'If we were as bad as the Koreans and the Japanese, we'd torture you."

The next day, they tortured me.

Now he is home, and he had these words to say at a celebration in his honor: "Now I've come home with the satisfaction of knowing

I served with honor. I have been met by the most beautiful and considerate wave of humanity ever. I accept the key to my hometown on behalf of the sons of this community and nation who, though they were unable to stand in this place of honor with me, today will stand in her heart forever. Thanks for your love and the very special way in which you have taken me into your heart and home. Seeing the display of American flags has brought me the warmest thrill, an immeasurable amount of pride—the quality I call Americanhood."

My family in Bladenboro received notice that I had been shot down and that my classification was "Missing in Action (MIA)/Probable Killed in Action" (KIA) because that's what other aircrews that witnessed my shoot down passed to Air Force intelligence when they were debriefed. Witnessing aircrews said, "Bridger's aircraft was struck directly by an SA-2 missile. It blew off the right wing, the left wing, and the tail. No one could have survived." They were also informed by a couple of USAF officers that Barry was lost and probably not coming home.

The population of Bladenboro at that time was about six hundred. It's now about 1,613, as of the 2019 census. When the word arrived in my hometown that I was shot down and that I was Missing in Action (MIA)/Probable Killed in Action (KIA), about half the people said, "Well, good grief, even Bridger could not have survived an explosion like that." The other half said, "Baloney! Bridger isn't dead."

Jim

Barry's sister-in-law, Sarah Bridger, the wife of his brother, McRae, said this about Barry being shot down:[19]

When we were informed that Barry was lost and probably not coming back, we were very sad but decided that we should do something. Mac and I got to work, and we started doing everything we

---

19 Phone interview with Sarah Bridger, June 19, 2019.

could to find Barry. It was common at that time for people to buy metal bracelets that had the name of the POW or MIA person from Vietnam. The idea behind the bracelets was to wear these until the person named on the bracelet came home. We sold these bracelets to raise money for these military personnel to contribute toward finding those who have not made it home. We also encouraged others to pray for his life since we did not know what happened to him. The Vietnamese Government refused to release the names of American POWs in their custody to gain leverage against selected POWs.

Barry
When they finally did release my name as a POW, the good folks of Bladenboro North Carolina had a party.

Jim
Sarah also recalled that she went to Washington with other women to let legislators know they wanted their loved ones back from Vietnam. She used to mail packages to Barry with cigars, medicine, cookies, and other items. But he never received them. She said, "The Vietnamese guards never gave the packages to the POWs. They took the cookies and either ate them or sold them."

Bracelets Worn While Waiting for Veterans to Return Home

An interesting cultural phenomenon that occurred during the Vietnam War was the wearing of POW bracelets, engraved with a service member's key identifying information. These bracelets were worn in honor of American prisoners of war. When a POW returned home, people would return their bracelets to the veteran and tell him they had worn it the entire time he was held captive.

In late 1969, a woman named Carol Bates Brown and a fellow college student, Kay Hunter, created POW bracelets as a way to remember American prisoners of war suffering in captivity in Southeast Asia. Brown became the National Chairman of the POW/MIA Bracelet Campaign for VIVA (Voices In Vital America), a Los Angeles-based student organization that produced and distributed the bracelets during the Vietnam War. Entertainers Bob Hope and Martha Raye served with her as honorary co-chairmen.[20]

Brown found an engraver in Santa Monica, California, who made twelve sample bracelets, engraved with each POW's name, rank, service, loss date, and country of loss. Brown and her team tried to find ways to fund production of the bracelets and were rebuffed by many, including Ross Perot. Here is Brown's recollection about the official launch of the bracelet program:[21]

On Veterans Day, November 11, 1970, they officially kicked off the bracelet program with a news conference at the Universal Sheraton Hotel. Public response quickly grew, and we eventually got to the point we were receiving over 12,000 requests a day. This also brought money in to pay for brochures, bumper stickers, buttons, advertising and whatever else we could do to publicize the POW/MIA issue. We formed a close alliance with the relatives of missing men -- they got bracelets from us on consignment and could keep some of the money they raised to fund their local organizations. We also tried to furnish these groups with all the stickers and other literature they could give away.

While Steve Frank and I ended up dropping out of college to work for VIVA full time to administer the bracelet and other POW/MIA programs, none of us got rich off the bracelets. VIVA's adult advisory group, headed by Gloria Coppin, was adamant that we would not have a highly paid professional staff. As I recall the highest salary was $15,000, a year and we were able to keep administrative costs to less than 20 percent of income.

In all, VIVA distributed nearly five million bracelets and raised enough money to produce untold millions of bumper stickers, buttons, brochures, matchbooks, newspaper ads, etc., to draw attention to the missing men. In 1976, VIVA closed its doors. By then the American

---

20　Carol Bates Brown, "History of the POW/MIA Bracelet," The Vietnam Veterans Memorial, http://thewall-usa.com/bracelet.asp.

21　Ibid.

public was tired of hearing about Vietnam and showed no interest in the POW/MIA issue.

Barry's niece, Jeanne Konitzer, who is McRae's younger daughter, said, "We all wore a bracelet with Barry's name on it. Some were made of sterling silver. When Barry married Sheila, I gave mine to her. Sheila now has a box of these bracelets that were sent to her."

Here is just part of Sheila's collection of bracelets the people of Bladenboro kept during the time Barry was held captive in the Hanoi Hilton in North Vietnam. These bracelets are all engraved with Barry's name and date of capture. Once Barry returned home, eventually many towns-people returned their bracelets to Sheila and Barry. This is a moving testament to the love, appreciation, and fondness the people of Barry's hometown held for him—"never forgotten."

Chapter 7

KEEP YOUR SENSE OF HUMOR, NO MATTER WHAT

Jim

Since I first met Barry more than thirty years ago, he taught me to live in the moment. Whatever he did, he did it with vigor, enthusiasm, humor, and a sense of purpose. Imagine if you were subjected to what Barry was, as described in the preceding chapters. Could you find strength, resolve, and forgiveness? Barry didn't know if he would ever return from those awful conditions, so he made the most of them.

Barry has never stopped making the most of his life, to this day. And he holds no resentment, hatred, or anger toward anyone for the hardship he endured. In fact, it is captivating to hear him tell these stories in person—often, he has his audiences erupting in laughter. It takes a remarkable person to recount such horrific experiences with such humor and perspective. Barry is one remarkable person.

Barry

When my North Vietnamese captors picked me up off the ground, I had blood all over my face and looked like I was probably going to die. I immediately began to pretend I was blind, that I could see just well enough to stumble around. This fake blindness served me well throughout the rest of my time in captivity.

Our captors put my copilot, Dave, and me in a Jeep and drove us directly to Heartbreak Hotel, which was the central prison torture center at Hỏa Lò Prison, better known as the Hanoi Hilton. They put me in a room by myself.

When Dave and I were captured, the North Vietnamese figured that the big guy was in charge of the aircraft. They took him into an interrogation, thinking he was the boss, when actually, I was. They tortured the heck out of him. I was in another cell and could hear his screams, but I couldn't help him.

Meanwhile, there was a tap on my wall. So I put my ear up against the wall. I heard an individual say, "Pilot, pilot."

I didn't have a clue who was tapping. I could only surmise that a Vietnamese individual was on the other side of the wall, and his English was limited, but he was trying to get me to talk to him. I was reluctant to do so because I didn't know what was really going on. Somebody could have been trying to set me up. So I was very reluctant to engage in a conversation with somebody whose identity I was unsure of. He tried that for a while, but I didn't answer him.

After they tortured Dave, the North Vietnamese opened my cell door and took me to the torture chamber. It was three years before I saw Dave again.

A Brief History of the Hanoi Hilton[22]

The name Hỏa Lò is commonly translated as "fiery furnace" or "hell's hole." The name originated from the street name Phố Hỏa Lò because of the concentration of stores selling wood coal-fired stoves along the street from pre-colonial times.

The French built the prison in Hanoi from 1886 to 1889 and from 1898 to 1901, when Vietnam was still part of French Indochina. The French called the prison "Maison Cen-

---

22   "Vietnamese Prison: Hanoi Hilton," Learning History, https://www.learning-history.com/vietnamese-prison-hanoi-hilton/.

trale"—Central House, a traditional euphemism that was used to refer to prisons in France. It was located near Hanoi's French Quarter. It was intended to hold Vietnamese prisoners, particularly political prisoners agitating for independence who were often subject to torture and execution.

A 1913 renovation expanded its capacity from 460 inmates to 600. Still, it was often overcrowded, holding some 730 prisoners on a given day in 1916, a figure that would rise to 895 in 1922 and 1,430 in 1933. By 1954, the prison held more than 2,000 people. With its inmates held in subhuman conditions, it became a symbol of colonialist exploitation and of the bitterness of the Vietnamese toward the French.

Following the defeat at the battle of Dien Bien Phu and the 1954 Geneva Accords, the French left Hanoi, and the prison came under the authority of the Democratic Republic of Vietnam. After that, the prison served as an education center for revolutionary doctrine and activity. After the French left, it was kept around to mark its historical significance to the North Vietnamese.

During the Vietnam War, the first US prisoner to be sent to Hỏa Lò was Lieutenant, Junior Grade Everett Alvarez Jr., who was shot down on August 5, 1964. From the beginning, US POWs endured miserable conditions, including poor food and unsanitary conditions.

American POWs sardonically nicknamed the prison complex the "Hanoi Hilton," in reference to the well-known Hilton Hotel chain. There is some disagreement among the first group of POWs who coined the name, but F8D pilot Bob Shumaker was the first to write it down, carving "Welcome to the Hanoi Hilton" on the handle of a pail to greet the arrival of Air Force Lieutenant Robert Peel.

My First Interrogation

Because I was pretending I couldn't see, I stumbled around, bumping into walls. I still had blood all over my face. Seated behind a table were three people: an interrogator we called Pig Eye and two MiG-21 fighter pilots from the North Vietnamese Air Force. We called the one guy Pig Eye because he had a red dot on his eyeball that went around and around in a circle like a crazy man.

The Mikoyan-Gurevich MiG-21 was a supersonic jet fighter and interceptor aircraft that was designed by the Mikoyan-Gurevich Design Bureau in the Soviet Union. They knew I was shot down in an F-4 Phantom. It was an aircraft they didn't like at all because the F-4 Phantoms shot down many of their aircraft.

The interrogator looked at me and said, "You must answer our questions."

I said, "No. I'll give you my name, rank, service number, and date of birth, as required by the Geneva Convention, but that's all."

About the Geneva Convention

The Geneva Convention was a series of international diplomatic meetings that produced several agreements, in particular the Humanitarian Law of Armed Conflicts, a group of international laws for the humane treatment of wounded or captured military personnel, medical personnel, and non-military civilians during war or armed conflicts. The agreements originated in 1864 and were significantly updated in 1949 after World War II.[23]

From the day that American airmen's feet touched the soil of North Vietnam, the government of that land declared all of us war criminals and summarily dismissed the benefits of the 1954 Geneva conventions to which we were entitled as uniformed, armed combatants. It was that easy for a nation that was a signatory to the 1954 Geneva Conventions—which prescribe the proper treatment of prisoners of war—to not only dismiss those benefits for American warriors and to do so throughout the duration of the conflict. Prisoners of war have an obligation to give name, rank, service number, and date of birth, and no more. But I was under no illusion that the government of North Vietnam would honor this obligation.

The Torture Begins

Upon capture, most of us experienced multiple torture sessions and interrogations that lasted for days or weeks. Within minutes of my arrival in Hanoi, I was taken to an interrogation and asked to give the name of my commanding officer. I reminded the interrogator that as a prisoner of war I was obligated to give only my name, rank, serial number, and date of birth. At that point, the interrogator we nicknamed Pig Eye left me with their chief torturer.

---

23 "Geneva Convention," History.com. https://www.history.com/topics/world-war-ii/geneva-convention.

We called him Lettuce Head because he always wore a metal helmet covered with leaves.

There were three basic tortures the Vietnamese liked to inflict on us. One was the straps, where the captors put your hands behind your back in manacles and laced up a fifteen- to twenty-foot parachute cord or strap, starting at your wrists. By the time they got to your neck, your shoulders were pulled out of the sockets.

A second method of torture was ratcheted "hell cuffs." They placed them on your wrists and ratcheted them down tight by placing your arms on the ground and stomping on the cuffs, causing them to cut into your flesh on both wrists. After about an hour, your hands were swollen up to the size of boxing gloves.

The third torture involved bamboo. The guards put your feet in locks so that your ankles were side by side. Then they would split a piece of bamboo in half. They would set one of the halves on top of your ankles and saw back and forth to cut into the flesh of your ankles.

There were other methods of torture, but any one of them was quite stimulating.

My first torture experience was with straps. Lettuce Head manacled my wrists behind my back, pulled my arms together from wrists to shoulders, and tried to pull my shoulders out of the sockets. He couldn't do it.

He became frustrated, so he left the room and came back with another guard. They put their feet on my back to hold me down, lifted my wrists off my back, and shoved my wrists toward my head. That tore my shoulders out of their sockets. Then they tightened the straps more so that my shoulders would not come back into the sockets, and they left the room. That was the technique they used. They wanted you to sit there alone, in incredible pain, and see how long you could last. Depending on who you were, you might last ten minutes, or you might last three hours, I'm sure most people couldn't calculate the time because they were so busy screaming.

Eventually, they came back, after what seemed like hours. They took the straps off and lowered my shoulders back into the sockets, injured and full of trauma that remains today.

Infuriating My Captors

At that point, I decided I would resort to what is known as a "classical second line of resistance." This meant that I pretended to cooperate by answering their questions without giving them any information.

Their first question to me was, "How fast can the F-4 fly?"

"I responded, "It is fast."

"The interrogator turned to his two MiG-21 pilots and said, "He says it's fast. They looked at the interrogator like he was crazy and said, "Well, how fast?"

He came back to me and asked, "How fast?"

I said, "Very fast."

He communicated that to the two MiG-21 pilots. I could see that they were getting agitated. He turned to me and said, "How many kilometers per hour? You must tell us how fast."

I said, "I am a junior pilot. I am not allowed to fly fast. I do not know."

He looked at me and said, "Damn." He turned to the MiG-21 pilots and said, "Sucker's a junior pilot. They don't allow him to fly fast." Then he said to me. "Oh, OK."

This interrogation was getting so damn funny. He went to the next question: "Can the F-4 fly in the clouds?"

The questions I was getting were sophomoric and comical. They made me want to play. I said, "No, you can't fly in the weather with an F-4 because you can't see."

They nodded their heads as if to say, "That sounds right."

I was almost enjoying the game because they didn't have a damn clue what they were doing.

Then one day, the interrogator said, "Now, you must write a confession."

Still pretending to be blind, I said, "I can't see."

"You must write a confession. You'll be severely punished if you do not."

I said, "No, I'm not going to do that." So I went back to the torture chamber. One classic line I remember the interrogator saying was, "If we were the Japanese fascists, or the German Nazi, we would torture you."

The next day, they tortured me again. Go figure!

Other Communists Interrogated Us, Too

The North Vietnamese invited Chinese, Cubans, and Russians in and out of the prison camps of North Vietnam. Some of them took part in interrogations and torture of American POWs.

After my week of torture, at around 11:00 p.m. or midnight, I was sitting in the interrogation room with Pig Eye. He got up, walked out of the room, and disappeared. A few moments later, the door opened, and in walked a very small man wearing a nondescript gray military uniform with no insignia. He sat down behind the table and looked at me. My brain was going, "Now, who is this guy? I know dang well he is not Vietnamese. What is he doing in here?" The small man sat down, reached into his vest pocket, and pulled out a pack of Lucky Strike cigarettes. In impeccable English, he said, "Would you like a cigarette?"

I said, "No, I don't smoke." He smiled, lit up a cigarette, put the pack back into his breast pocket, looked at me, and said, "I have only a couple of questions."

I was thinking, "Now, who am I up against? Who is this guy? How much does he know? With the way he speaks English, he probably knows a heck of a lot."

He said, "My first question is, how many tracking G's can you pull with the F-4 Phantom and shoot sparrow missiles off AFT stations 5 and 6?"

He was trying to gain some strategic information on the flight characteristics of the F-4 Phantom, to help the MiG-21 pilots in North Vietnam have a better chance of killing some F-4 aircraft.

I thought, "Oh, crap."

Right before I was shot down, I had just learned the answer to that question regarding the latest update on the F-4 missile systems and g-forces. He was asking me an important question. At certain g-forces[24], the F-4 should not fire missiles; they won't track. That was a very important piece of information, and I was blown away when he asked me that question so precisely.

---

24 Here is an explanation of g-forces in the context of flying fighter jets from Sky and Space Travel at https://www.skyandspacetravel.com/speed_gforce.html: "When you fly fighter jets, you must consider G-forces, or G-load—a numerical ratio of any applied force to the gravitational force at the Earth's surface. This is a force that acts on a body as a result of acceleration or gravity and is described in units of acceleration equal to one G. For example, a 10-pound object undergoing a G-force of 5 G experiences 50 pounds of force. The force of gravity on Earth is used as a baseline for measuring these forces of acceleration. As you pull more Gs, your weight increases accordingly."

I pretended that I didn't understand tracking from Adam. I replied, "Tracking what?"

He smiled instantly because he knew damn well that I was pulling his leg. Then he abruptly stood up and said, "Either you do not know the answer to my questions, or you do not want to share it with me. It doesn't matter."

As he left the room, I was wondering, "Who the heck was that?" I have no doubt that he was a Chinese intelligence officer. No doubt.

The Cubans also conducted a detailed interrogation-training program to teach the Vietnamese how to extract information from American POWs without torture. A year later, when their program failed, the Cubans resorted to torture themselves. The Vietnamese eventually lost confidence in their program and sent them home.

Finally, They Think I Have Confessed

After seven days of torture and interrogations, Pig Eye came in and put a piece of paper and a pen down. He demanded a confession again. I am right-handed, so I don't write well with my left hand. Purposely, I wrote with my left hand so my penmanship would be poor. I also wrote gibberish—words that didn't relate to each other. They made no logical sense whatsoever. Here's an example of what I wrote:

I am but you can I will Not quick but there it is.

You see—absolutely unintelligible gibberish.

Other POWs wrote similar things that had no meaning. A fellow POW wrote one of my favorites:

I have a pet electric duck.
When you wind it up,
it flies around the room
and goes quack, quack, quack.

These so-called confession documents extracted over years of abuse and brutal torture provided many of my fellow POWs with the last laugh. After my week in the Heartbreak Hotel torture center, the North Vietnamese camp authority put me in an isolated cell in an area of the prison we called New-Guy Village. This area was reserved for new POWs who had completed initial torture and interrogations. I still had a bloody-looking head.

A Close Call with a Penicillin Shot That Would Have Killed Me

The next morning, the door opened, and in walked a Vietnamese wearing a white smock. He appeared to be a nurse, and he had a needle in his hand. I knew what he was thinking: "This guy has a bloody head, and he's been tortured, so we need to give him a shot." I guessed penicillin. He motioned for me to roll up my shirtsleeve so he could give me the shot.

I am deathly allergic to penicillin, and I was trying to figure out how to communicate to this idiot that if he were to give me a shot of penicillin, it could kill me. So I took my hand and waved it back and forth in front of him, saying, "No, no!" He looked at me sternly and said what probably was something like, "You've got to do what we say, not what you want to do. Now, roll up your damn shirtsleeve."

I realized that he didn't understand what I was trying to tell him. He thought I was just being obstinate. So I took my thumb and three fingers of my right hand, put them on my left shoulder, and then ran my fingers down my arm, saying, "Puff, puff, puff!" I was trying to simulate hives popping up on my skin. Then he realized what I was telling him. He said, "Oh! Oh!" He turned around and left. At least he was smart enough to get the point that I was allergic to penicillin.

The North Vietnamese Call My Bluff

I took the idea of pretending to be blind and parlayed it into a convincing narrative that I couldn't see well enough to write. That was my technique, and it seemed to work well until one day an interrogator opened my peephole and asked, "Have you written a biography?"

I said, "Yes, I wrote a biography, a good one!"

He left. About four days later, he came by, opened the peephole, and said, "You sure you write biography?"

I said, "Yes, I wrote a biography. You must have lost it."

The next day, he came back and said, "You no write biography. Now we take you to hospital and if you lie about your eyes, you will be severely punished."

The camp authority had decided to call my bluff.

They handcuffed me, put me in the Jeep, and drove me to a hospital in downtown Hanoi. At that point, things were getting dicey. They took me out of the Jeep, and we went up to a room on the second story. I wish I had some video of that room. It was incredibly dark, but I could see that the ceiling was about ten feet high. At one end of the room, there was a chair and a desk. At the other end of the room, there was a set of black drapes from the ceiling down to the floor.

The guards sat me down in the chair. The interrogator sat down behind me at the desk. The interrogator said, "Now we examine your eyes, and if you lie, you'll be severely punished."

About that time, just like in a Laurel and Hardy movie, into the room walked this technician in a white smock with a great big eyepiece wrapped around his head. He had a long stick in his hand that looked like a pool cue. He took the curtain and moved it from right to left, exposing an eye chart. At the very top of the chart was the letter E. It was huge—about three feet tall.

The camp authority had decided to give me an eye test. The medical assistant stood there with that pool cue, pointing at the large E. The interrogator said, "Now, you must tell us what you see."

I turned toward the interrogator and said, "What is it I'm supposed to be looking at?"

Now, if you had any vision at all, you couldn't miss this white-smocked guy with the pool stick and the chart with the huge E. But I was pretending that I didn't see anything. Swiveling in my chair from left to right, I said, "Where is it? Where do you want me to look?" As I carried on with that, the white-smocked guy was pounding the stick on the chart in different places. I said, "Where is he? What am I supposed to be looking at? Where is he?"

Finally, the interrogator got so damn irritated that he said to the guy with the pool stick, "Come back here and look into his eyes up close."

The assistant approached me with what looked like a magnifying glass. He placed it in front of my face. I responded by blinking my eyes as fast as I could, as if I had an uncontrollable, impulsive vibration in my face, around my eyes. After I did that for about three minutes, everybody became exasperated. They marched me downstairs, put me in the Jeep, drove me back to my cell, and left me alone.

Years later, while my fellow POWs were sunning in our courtyard, I remained in our large room to practice my juggling. Unbeknownst to me, the same interrogator who had called my bluff about my bad eyes years earlier was watching my juggling practice through an open door.

I had five balls in the air when he walked in, screaming, "You lie, you lie, you lie!"

I let all the balls fall to the floor, turned to him, pointed to my eyes, and in a forceful and regretful tone, I said, "No lie. Used to juggle ten, now only five."

I pointed to my eyes and said, "I cannot see."

The interrogator's face said it all: "That poor American used to juggle ten balls, now only five. So sad!"

We were all doing this kind of stuff, deriving great satisfaction out of deceiving our captors.

Biography Torture

America's Vietnam POWs started off typically in solitary confinement for a few months to a year. I was in solitary confinement for about six months before I received a roommate. That was the good news. The bad news was, I was challenged once again by the camp authority that I had not written a biography. They immediately took me to the torture chamber to force the issue.

The interrogator placed pen and paper in front of me and demanded that I write a biography. I refused! America's Vietnam POWs sardonically committed themselves to remaining in the torture chamber as long as possible to deny its use by a fellow POW. It was my turn once again.

The interrogator ordered two bricks to be placed on the floor. I was then directed to place a knee on each brick and raise my hands over my head. If I failed to hold that position, I would be beaten back into position. This self-torture would cease only if I wrote the biography! After observing me for a few minutes, the interrogator and guards departed the room, locking the door behind them. I observed that the door had multiple locks, and it took about twenty seconds to open it. So I immediately stood up and discovered the door had built-in shutters that allowed one to look out but not into the room.

I was able to monitor activity outside my door, giving me the time to re-establish my position on the bricks if required. I made one huge mistake! I failed to realize there was a window in the back of the room. While I was focused on front-door activity, the window came open. I was caught! Although I was able to quickly re-establish my position on the bricks, I expected consequences. I wasn't disappointed. The interrogator ordered a guard to hit me on my knee with a 2x4. Lucky for me, the guard hit me with the flat side of the 2x4, creating more sound than pain. The interrogator said to me, "How was that?"

Without thinking, I replied, "Not bad."

Bad idea! The guard was admonished and ordered to hit me again with the narrow side of the 2x4, producing little sound and much pain. "Was that better?" the interrogator asked.

I responded, "Absolutely."

It turned out that the window was a blessing. It, like the door, had built-in shutters with the same viewing configuration. I reasoned that if I could get to the window without detection, I might be able to see an approaching guard with the time necessary to re-establish myself on the bricks. If true, I could rely on my ears to detect a front-door threat and my eyes to detect a window threat at the same time and still have sufficient time to re-establish myself on the bricks. My first challenge was getting to the window the first time.

When the torturers left my room the second time, I knew I would have to wait for the window to open at least twice. This meant about thirty to forty minutes on the bricks. My timing worked. The question now was, how long could I stay on my feet to sustain this charade? I spent the next five days and nights at that window. I fell asleep on the sixth day and celebrated on the seventh by once again creating an unreadable, unintelligible document laced with gibberish.

Talk about Fun! Tormenting Our Captors

Tormenting our captors got kind of funny at times.

One Sunday night during the period when torture was rampant, I was sitting in my little one-man cell. It was 114 to 118 degrees in my cell because in the summertime, those masonry buildings soaked up heat from the sun all day long and radiated it into the room all night long. I sat in the cell covered with a bleeding heat rash. Because it was a Sunday night, all the guards were on liberty, except one. I was bored to tears, so I decided to do something. I made the sound of a wild-turkey gobble.

Instantly, I heard the patter of feet outside in the courtyard as the guard ran into our cellblock. The physical structure of our cellblock was a long hallway with 5x7-foot individual solitary confinement cells on both sides. I heard him open the peephole to the first cell. He looked in and tried to imitate my turkey call. The response by my fellow POW was predictable: "No, he** no! Not me—baloney!"

He continued down the hallway, opening the peephole to every cell, trying to convince a POW to admit that he was the one making the noises. When he opened my peephole, I just pointed to the next cell. He looked at me like, "Really? OK. It's the next guy."

This time, he opened the door to my room's adjoining cell and beat the heck out of my buddy, Bob, slammed the door, and pranced back to his duty station, quite proud of himself. About five minutes later, I heard a tap rhythm of "shave and a haircut" on my wall. I answered with a tap rhythm of two bits. That's how we initiated communications with the tap code. Bob wanted to talk! I put my ear to the wall, and Bob began to tap. He was upset, made threats of bodily harm to me, and said he was going to do some things to me that I knew were physically impossible.

I thought, "Well, that's very rude."

After he quit his tirade, I tapped to him and said, "Bob, I do not appreciate your comments. Your mother would be disappointed in you. Your language is unbecoming of a military officer. You are overreacting. So, if you don't apologize to me right now for what you said, I'm going to make that bird call again."

There was a pregnant pause. Bob tapped back, "I'm sorry, you *sun* b***h."

When we got out of Hanoi, Bob didn't kill me. I got him a date with one of the best-looking and wealthiest ladies in Wilmington, North Carolina. He was happy as a lark.

It was incredibly fun to mess with our captors. If you try hard enough, you can find the humor in any situation. In fact, humor will help you *endure* even the most horrific situation.

Chapter 8

ALWAYS LOOK FOR NEW WAYS TO DO THINGS

Jim

People who have endured long-term confinement, like Barry did, often say the worst part of that experience is isolation from other people. As human beings, we need to be connected with one another. The North Vietnamese who ran the "Hanoi Hilton" did everything they could to keep their POWs from communicating because they wanted to compound their suffering. But they were no match for the innovative, fast-thinking, and tenacious American POWs.

In this chapter, Barry recounts some of the innovative ways he and his fellow POWs communicated, despite their captors' best efforts to isolate them. His story shows us that we should always look for new ways to do things. When Plan A doesn't work out, move to Plan B.

Barry
Our Lifeline: Communicating via Code

The quality of our lives rested heavily on communication.

Newly captured POWs were invariably placed in cells away from the general POW population. They didn't want the new guys to have the support of the old heads. As a POW body, our biggest problem was developing safe and effective communications among cells, cellblocks, and buildings. The strength of our resistance and the quality of our lives rested heavily on communication. The North Vietnamese camp authority often said, "We will sever your communication links, and effective resistance will wither on the vine."

Our Captors Moved Us to Disrupt Our Ability to Communicate

Their favorite technique to attack our communication systems was to move us around from cell to cell, cellblock to cellblock, prison camp to prison camp. Moving us around was their trump card. They also placed American POWs in prison camps close to the Chinese border to facilitate their rapid movement into China to complicate potential rescue efforts by US Special Forces. We were their bargaining chip.

All the POWs were in solitary confinement cells, but we developed communication techniques that allowed us to talk from room to room and to pass messages from one cellblock across a courtyard to another cellblock. When you're in a place for months or years, you figure out ways to do that. Moving us around kept us from being efficient in communicating with one another, and movement happened all the time.

During my six and a half years in Hanoi, I was in seven or eight different prisons. That was true for most of us. I spent the longest period at Hỏa Lò Prison, the central prison in downtown Hanoi sardonically named the "Hanoi Hilton" by America's Vietnam POWs.

A Note Appears in My Rice

POWs from the general prison population were responsible for placing food, twice a day, on a table for the American POWs in New Guy Village (NGV). The food plates were arranged in such a way that you could pick up only the top plate. The order in which NGV POWs picked up their food was established by the camp authority and rigidly enforced. Controlling the food-plate choice and knowing the order of pickup by new POWs allowed notes to be passed to specific POWs in NGV. This created an important communication channel between new POWs and our senior leadership.

One evening, I discovered a note buried in my rice with specific instructions on the structure and use of the American Vietnam POW tap code. I thought, "What the heck is this?"

The tap code was made up of twenty-five letters (five rows and five columns) with the letters "c" and "k" used interchangeably. Message context usually confirmed which letter was intended, but not always.

For example, one day, someone tapped to me and said, "Jim F-A-C-E-S blindness." For three days, I prayed for Jim. Then one day, it dawned on me, "Wait a minute, that may be F-A-K-E-S." I went to the wall and tapped, "What's really going on with Jim?"

Jim tapped back, "I'm fine, faking, not facing."

Down at the bottom, the note said, "All POWs, learn this code." Look and listen for this code in many ways. It also cautioned me that the "fuzz" also knows this code. Use of the word fuzz removed any doubt I had that the note came from our ranks. It concluded with, "Destroy this note."

I ate the note.

Smitty Harris's Book, *Tap Code*

Jim

In November 2019, the book *Tap Code* was published. It recounts the experiences of Carlyle Smith "Smitty" Harris, who was the sixth American POW captured in the air war over North Vietnam on April 4, 1965.

In the book *Tap Code*, Smitty Harris recalls how he was reunited with some fellow POWs after being in solitary confinement for an extended period of time. Harris learned the Tap Code from Sergeant Claude Watkins in 1963 during Escape and Evasion school in Nevada. The Sergeant explained that a POW used the Tap Code in Germany to communicate with his comrades by tapping on a water pipe. The code is much easier to use than Morse code because it contains no dashes.

So Harris taught the code to his comrades for "possible future use." He noted that with two sets of taps, the POWs could identify the column and row that designated any letter of the alphabet. As Barry explained, the code is a five-by-five matrix of the alphabet, excluding the letter K:[25]

	1	2	3	4	5
1	A	B	C	D	E
2	F	G	H	I	J
3	L	M	N	O	P
4	Q	R	S	T	U
5	V	W	X	Y	Z

Harris shares that long after the Vietnam War was over, he visited one of his fellow POWs, Bud Day, as he lay dying. Day was awarded the Medal of Honor and became a lawyer, fighting for veterans' rights and benefits. That day, as they visited for the last time, Day said to Harris, "Smitty, I want to thank you for introducing the Tap Code. It made all the difference in our communications network and was a lifeline for all of us." Then Day took Harris's hand and tapped on the back of his hand the CODE GBU: "God bless you."[26]

The tap code was an extremely powerful means of POW communication because of its versatility. It could be employed as long as you could use your senses to make or detect repetitive motion. To select letters, you would tap down to the correct row and over to the proper column. The tap sequence for the word HI would be TAP, TAP pause TAP, TAP, TAP (H) TAP, TAP pause

---

25   Carlyle S. Harris and Sara W. Berry, *Tap Code: The Epic Survival Tale of a Vietnam POW and the Secret Code That Changed Everything*, Kindle edition (Grand Rapids, Michigan: Zondervan, 2019), 112–14.

26   Ibid., 255.

TAP, TAP, TAP, TAP (I): i.e. (HI). You could also send the word HI while sweeping the courtyard. It would work like this: BRUSH, BRUSH, pause BRUSH, BRUSH, BRUSH (H) BRUSH, BRUSH, pause BRUSH, BRUSH, BRUSH, BRUSH (I).

Creating and detecting repetitive motion was the key. The tap code was dangerous to use and very slow. The guards were always listening in on our walls. With the shootdown and capture of USAF Lt. Tom McNish, America's Vietnam POW communications system experienced a profound revolution. Shortly after his arrival, he developed and introduced to his fellow POWs what he called the American Vietnam POW hand code, which he modeled after the deaf-mute code.

The letters of the deaf-mute code are small and designed to be read at close range. The POW hand code is composed of big letters designed to be read at a distance. Good eyes were in demand to become an American aviator and invaluable to reaping the rewards of this new POW hand code. Although the POW hand code could not and did not replace the tap code, it was lightning-fast, extremely secure, and greatly enhanced the quality of our lives.

We called the POW tap code "analog communications"—very effective, but dangerous and slow. Contrast that with the POW hand code, which we called "digital communications"—lightning-fast and very secure.

Snapping Shirts to Communicate

The morning after I ate my note, I saw an American walking along the edge of my cellblock. He had a shirt and a bucket. He walked up to a well, dropped the bucket into the water, and retrieved a bucket of water. He put the shirt into the bucket of water and began to wash it. He looked toward my room purposefully because he knew darn well there was a new American POW in New Guy Village.

He took the shirt out of the bucket, wrung it out, and started popping it. *Pop, pop, pop*—he kept popping that shirt. The Vietnamese guard was standing there with his pig sticker, ignoring everything.

I wondered, "What the heck is that Yank doing?"

He started over: snap, snap, pause, snap, pause, snap snap snap snap snap snap snap snap snap snap snap snap snap snap snap.

Not receiving the reaction he expected, he hit the right side of his head with his hand, as if to say, "Dummy!"

Then he started all over: 1 snap, 123 snaps, and ended with a bunch of snaps. I thought, "That doesn't make any sense." Then it dawned on me: "It's not 1-2-3; it's the alphabet—A, B, C…it's C-A-N." He was trying to say to me, "Can you read, dummy?"

I coughed, which meant, "Yep. I got it."

We convinced the Vietnamese guards that the way Americans dried their clothes was to snap them dry. *Snap, snap.* But we were really sending code. Each series of snaps ended on a letter of the alphabet. They thought we were just drying our clothes because we told them, "This is how we dry our clothes in America—we snap them." We also communicated code while coughing. The guards never realized that we were coding all around them.

This was an example of the way that we established contact with new POWs. We had to take risks to get them into the system. In my case, they did it two ways. They passed a note in my rice, and the POW popping his shirt demonstrated the importance of looking and listening for the American POW tap code in many different ways.

Always Inventing New Ways to Communicate

We had all kinds of techniques for passing communication from one room in a cellblock to another cellblock.

For example, over a period of time, we were able to train everybody with the POW tap code. We started making tools to allow us to drill holes in the soft concrete walls of the Hanoi Hilton prison. We made concrete plugs to hide those holes. We removed these plugs to clear the area around our cellblocks before communicating.

We even had air-mail delivery. We would make, out of brick dust, a type of ink and, using a bamboo pen, write a message on a piece of paper. Then we'd secure it to a rock. Using the POW cough code, we would alert American POWs in the courtyard of an adjacent building to clear their area. When ready to receive message, we would cough "Clear to send." Then we'd throw the message into their courtyard. Using a pre-agreed-on code, the receiving POWs would acknowledge the throw as a success or failure.

Well, one day, my buddy, Ed Davis, now deceased, bless his soul, made a bad, bad throw. The rock landed between the two buildings, visible to anyone passing by. So we threw Ed over the courtyard wall and made him go get it. He was very quick, and we didn't get in trouble.

The 1976 book *POW: A Definitive History of the American Prisoner-of-War Experience in Vietnam, 1964–1973* by John Hubbell contains the best description of how we communicated and the hand signals we used to communicate with. My wife, Sheila, and our daughters know and use this code. We communicate with it all the time; it's easy to use. Everybody should know this code.

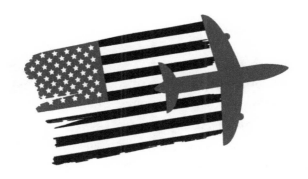

Chapter 9

HOLD TO YOUR VALUES TO OVERCOME YOUR GREATEST CHALLENGES

Jim

Do you find it difficult to deal with life's obstacles? Do you find yourself wanting to give up when the going gets rough? Certainly, we are all faced with challenges that are beyond our control. Sometimes, it helps to understand that no matter how difficult your circumstances are, there is always someone who has to overcome something worse than you.

So the next time you think you just can't deal with whatever is confronting you, think about what Barry and his fellow POWs endured. Figure out what your values are, and hold onto them tightly as you look for solutions.

Barry

In the prison camps of Southeast Asia, America's warriors were subjected to bizarre physical and psychological pressures. In the early years of imprisonment, we faced primarily physical pressures. The psychological dragons did not raise their ugly heads until the third, fourth, and fifth years of internment, depending on how we were put together between the ears.

Physical Pressures

The North Vietnamese used a combination of physical pressures to optimize our discomfort. Here are the primary ways they accomplished this:

1. **Torture:** In terms of physical pressures, torture was number one.
2. **Harassment:** Systematic and continuous process of abuse was second.
3. **Solitary confinement:** For most of us, solitary confinement lasted months. For a select few, it lasted years. But we had so many clever communication techniques, it was a bit like having a private room.
4. **Living conditions:** Living conditions for us in Hanoi were not great. We had no books, no pencils, no paper, no medical care, and too often inadequate food, exercise, and sleep. But compared with the circumstances faced by American and Allied POWs in the jungles of Southeast Asia, we were far better off.

Psychological Pressures

Our captors compounded our physical discomfort by adding the following psychological pressures to our daily lives:

1. **Threat of torture.** The number one physical pressure was torture. It was always lurking just around the corner. If you have seen film or video footage of an American in a North Vietnamese press conference, let me share how the North Vietnamese Communist orchestrated those charades. The participating members of the press were given a set of questions they could read to the POW in sequence, or they were

not allowed at the table. The American POW was brutally tortured to memorize the answers in sequence. The torturers were always standing behind the stage curtain with their torture implements as a grim reminder to the American as he walked out not to stray from the memorized answers. This was deadly, bloody-serious business, and you did not want to be that American.

2. **Fear of removal.** We had one American POW who was so badly tortured he lost touch with reality. The North Vietnamese refused to accept his psychotic circumstances. They called him "the faker." We had to hold this young man down on a concrete bed twice a day and cut off the airflow through his nose to force him to breathe through his mouth so that we could cram food down his throat to keep him alive. We were not about to let this American warrior die while we could care for him.

   A couple of times a month, the guards would drag this young man to the center courtyard, tie him to a tree, and beat him unmercifully with a rubber hose. They had one objective: they wanted him to open his mouth and say anything. On one occasion, the guard hit him in the face with that rubber hose. The remarkable thing about that incident was not the welt left around the POW's face, but the fact that when he was struck, he never blinked his eyes. This young man did not know who he was or where he was, and he was completely oblivious to pain. Then one day, the camp authority came and took him away. He never came back. He was removed.

3. **The anguish of possibly dishonoring our country.** The North Vietnamese camp authority reasoned that if they could force an American to do that which he desperately did not want to do, then the American would not have the heart to bounce back. Between torture sessions, when I was all alone, I made my way to an old desktop. As I gazed at the top of that desk, I saw a message that had been written by an American. You couldn't miss it. It had been permanently chiseled into the wood. It read, "May God and my country forgive me for what I have done."

My first reaction was to say to myself, "What on earth could you have done?" Then I realized, here was an American who had created for himself a set of standards and ideas by which he intended to live his life, but in his judgment, he had failed to measure up. In his grief, he had written this very public and chilling message of atonement.

4. **Boredom.** Boredom was a psychological pressure that we handled very well. We were a well-educated group, and when we weren't dodging the torture chambers, we spent endless hours sharing information on every topic from home construction to thermodynamics.

   At the end of the conflict, we had American Vietnam POWs returning to the universities all across this great land, taking the final exams in courses that spanned the sciences, humanities, and arts and receiving full credit, all of which they learned by tapping to each other through a three--foot-thick concrete wall in POW code.

5. **Loss of contact with family/loved ones.** We had always agreed among ourselves that the bombardment of North Vietnam would never cease without an agreement to release us. Then one day, the bombs stopped falling, but we were still there. It was also at this time that some of our men received letters of divorce. Do you suppose the camp authority shared these letters to all the POWs? You bet. These letters read pretty much the same: "Dear Ben, it has been four long years, and the girls and I still do not know if you are even alive. I have to make some horrible decisions because we have to go on. I have obtained a divorce. May God forgive me."

   Now, I am not pointing fingers at the government or the families. Those were trying and difficult times for everyone, but under those conditions, you can appreciate why some of our men began to feel terribly alone and abandoned.

6. **The worry of contracting a contagious disease or dying.** The psychological pressure that bugged me the most was the possibility of contracting a contagious disease and becoming crippled or dying before I could make it home. I was a single guy and did not have the pressures associated with having a wife and children. But that was an

extremely unhealthy place to live. We had great Americans who died within forty-eight hours with typhoid fever and multiple interrogators who died with malaria. We needed to leave.

Why/How Did We Endure?

Words cannot be assembled that capture in full measure the horror of war, the pain, the scars, and the sacrifice regarding why and how America's veterans have always been able to endure the crucible of war and return with honor. I believe the answer lies in what we Americans value about life, about living, about being.

Values are the rules by which a nation and its people live their lives. Your deeply held beliefs, therefore, define who you are and how you are likely to behave. Jesus of Nazareth put it this way: "As you believe, so shall it be done unto you."

The American Vietnam prisoner of war experience is therefore not a story about the plight of American POWs serving in the prison camps of Southeast Asia nearly so much as it is a revelation of the power of traditional American values.

I talk a lot about American values because in the prison camps of North Vietnam, I was a witness to the powerful and pervasive impact that traditional American values had on my fellow POWs to not only engage but to survive the pressure-cooker environment of the Hanoi Hilton. If you were captured by the North Vietnamese, you were placed into a concrete box. You had no idea what was about to happen. You were all alone with your thoughts and your values. Eventually, you were taken to an interrogation and given two choices: cooperate fully with the North Vietnamese camp authority or go to the torture chamber. Without any idea what their fellow POWs had done, one by one, all of America's POWs exercised the values they held in common and chose the torture chamber.

Once again, the world was reminded that you can imprison American warriors with brick and steel, but you cannot shackle their resolve to live in harmony with the values of their ancestors.

The question our veterans encounter the most often about their combat service is, "What, pray tell, would I have done under the brutal pressure of combat, the brutal of serious physical or psychological injury, or the brutal pressure of a POW camp?"

The answer, of course, would have been predetermined by the values you brought to the fight. You are what you value. You will take out what you took in. If you enter a period of great tribulation focused on yourself, you are very likely to come out even more self-centered. On the other hand, if you enter a period of great travail focused on ideas that are more meaningful, more lasting, and ultimately more human—ideas such as faith, family, friends, service to others, and doing those things that are truly worth remembering—then you are likely to come out with a deeper, more profound commitment to these enduring life principles.

In a POW camp, war is every day. You quickly learn that you cannot be a POW of one. Our survival was dependent on the help we received from one another. Conversely, our spiritual well-being, our sense of inner peace, and our personal commitment were not dependent on the help we received but on the help we were willing to give. I personally was most at peace in our long, dark night of terror in prayer or helping someone in greater need than myself.

Our value system compelled us to act and thereby to survive.

The Escape

The brutal and unbridled torture of American POWs began in 1966 with the Hanoi march and ended with the opening of Camp Faith in July 1970. The abuse, however, never stopped.

In May 1969, US Air Force Captain John Dramesi and Captain Ed Atterberry made a daring escape attempt from the "Zoo Annex" prison in Hanoi The two men planned to break out of the camp disguised as Vietnamese peasants, steal a *sampan*, and paddle down the Red River to the Gulf of Tonkin, where they hoped to be picked up by the US Navy. Escaping from the prison proved to be the easiest part of the mission, but the two men never fully considered how they would be able to travel more than 110 miles through hostile, heavily populated territory to the coast. The fact that neither man was of Asian heritage nor spoke Vietnamese compounded their difficulties.

The two men escaped from the compound at night by crawling through an attic above the cells and climbing down the roof of the facility to the street. A North Vietnamese patrol discovered the two men at sunup the next day in a bramble thicket about four miles from the Zoo Annex. Captain Atterbury was tortured to death. Unbelievably, Captain Dramesi survived.

Over the course of the next two months, the prison authorities severely tortured dozens of American POWs. One officer, Lieutenant Eugene "Red" McDaniel, received seven hundred lashes, as well as electric shocks and a form of rope torture during the ordeal, which he called his "darkest hour."

Dramsei and Atterberry's Ill-Fated Attempt to Escape

Jim

The following account of the two captains' attempt to escape appeared in a 1999 issue of *Air Force Magazine*:[27]

Air Force Capt. John A. Dramesi, who was captured April 2, 1967, was determined to escape despite the odds. The pugnacious former star high school wrestler and son of a boxer had already tried to escape en route to Hanoi. For months, he and fellow conspirators squirreled away string, wire, and bamboo that could be used for tools or weapons. Donated scraps of food were hidden in a cache. They gathered straw, thread, and cloth to weave civilian attire. Conical peasant hats were fabricated from rice straw taken from sleeping mats. Dramesi acquired brown iodine pills for water purification and to help darken the skin color of those attempting to escape. On May 10, 1969, Dramesi and Air Force Capt. Edwin L. Atterberry advised the leadership, "We're going tonight."

They did. Dramesi calculated that, by dawn, they had traveled four or five miles from the compound. But that was it. A North Vietnamese patrol found the pair hiding in a bramble thicket near an abandoned churchyard. The two were captured, blindfolded and handcuffed, and returned to prison. Dramesi was tortured for 38 days, flogged with a fan belt, punched, strapped into excruciating positions by ropes, and kept awake. He was strung in the ropes 15 times. Eventually he broke.

27   "Honor Bound," Stewart M. Powell, *Air Force Magazine*, August 1, 1999, https://www. airforcemag.com/article/0899honor/.

In a horror chamber close to Dramesi, the communists tortured Atterberry so grue-somely that his shrieks of pain could be heard two blocks away. Atterberry died on May 18, 1969, just eight days after the breakout.

The communists didn't stop with punishing Dramesi and Atterberry. They tortured other prisoners-some for weeks-who had not participated in the escape attempt and even extended the torture to other prisons.

"So traumatic had been the overall experience that even when escape became a more feasible option late in the captivity, the prisoners were still haunted by the catastrophic consequences of the Dramesi-Atterberry attempt," the historians wrote.

The consequences of the escape for the rest of us were wide-ranging, brutal, and long-lasting. In the Zoo Annex where the escape originated, the Communist Party, wearing gray uniforms and no insignia, replaced the military and began a purge. They had three objectives: identify every American POW who was connected in any way with the escape, compare testimony from participating POWs derived from torture and interrogations until they were confident they understood every aspect of the escape, and selectively torture non-participants to send a message that the brutal consequences of an escape attempt by a few would be shared by all.

I was a POW in the Zoo Annex for the months leading up to and after the escape. I had eight roommates, and we were unaware of any aspect of the escape attempt. Our first indication was a frantic tap-code communication from the adjacent room in our building, which told us that the Vietnamese had broken all our communication codes and to be aware. Shortly thereafter, the guards instructed me to put on a long-sleeved shirt and pants. My wrists were then manacled in front of my body. The outside air temperature was already in the 90s. Bleeding heat rash quickly covered my body. The guards also papered over every ventilation duct to our cells, turning our rooms into saunas. Room temperatures soared and remained well over 100 degrees from May 1969 until Ho's death in September 1969.

Over time, we learned that one or more POWs in every room were being constrained. It was clear that the camp authority would selectively torture non-participants to send the message that the brutal consequences of an escape attempt by a few would indeed be shared by all. What my fellow POWs and I did not know was that the pain and suffering of this classic example of slow torture would last almost six months.

Ho Chi Minh's Death Brings Hope

In the spring of 1969, the International Red Cross roundly and soundly condemned the government of North Vietnam for its mistreatment of American POWs. In the fall of 1969, the leader of the North Vietnamese government and people, Ho Chi Minh, died. America's Vietnam POWs would agree that the cross we had to bear was Ho. He was a vindictive, miserable old man who could not take it out on Uncle Sam, so he took it out on America's Vietnam prisoners of war.

The death of Ho Chi Minh provided the government with a wonderful opportunity to change policy. They did. It was profound. But let me add perspective with three questions: Did we ever receive the benefits of the Geneva Convention? No! Did we ever see the Red Cross? No! Did we have men going legally blind for a lack of simple vitamins? Yes! In November 1969, my manacles were removed, room vents were reopened, and the slow-torture program terminated. We held our breath, praying that our long, dark night of terror was over.

Ho Chi Minh, Communist Leader Striving to Unify Vietnam[28]

Ho Chi Minh first emerged as an outspoken voice for Vietnamese independence while living as a young man in France during World War I. Inspired by the Bolshevik Revolution; he joined the Communist Party and traveled to the Soviet Union. He helped found the Indochinese Communist Party in 1930 and the League for the Independence of Vietnam, or Viet Minh, in 1941.

At the end of World War II, Viet Minh forces seized the northern Vietnamese city of Hanoi and declared a Democratic State of Vietnam (North Vietnam) with Ho as president. Known as "Uncle Ho," he served in that position for the next twenty-five years, becoming a symbol of Vietnam's struggle for unification during a long and costly conflict with the strongly anti-Communist regime in South Vietnam and its powerful ally, the United States.

---

28   "Ho Chi Minh," History.com, https://www.history.com/topics/vietnam-war/ho-chi-minh-1.

Chapter 10

MAKE EVERY DAY A GOOD DAY BY CONTROLLING YOUR MIND

Jim

Imagine being in confinement for a day, a week, a month, or a year. It would be difficult for the most persistent among us. Barry lived a good portion of his life in confinement by this point of his life, in the orphanage and then in the POW camp. As he explains in this chapter, the POWs entertained themselves by using their brains, bodies, and hearts. Each of these heroes endured much, and those who made it out alive were transformed forever.

I consider the lesson in this chapter to be one of the most inspiring of all I have learned from this American hero. As Barry teaches us, you can make every day a good day by controlling your mind.

Barry

One skill I carried with me from life at the orphanage was the ability to entertain myself. At the orphanage, we had nothing to entertain us except a chinaberry tree, our brains, our bodies, and our hearts.

When people ask me what it was like in Hanoi, I say, "Well, in Hanoi, we had no pencils, no paper, no books, no medical care, and too often, inadequate food, sleep, and solitary confinement which lasted for months, sometime years—nothing!"

We were living in filthy conditions, with heat rash, bleeding sores, sickness, and toadstools growing out of our ears. Our cells were a playground for snakes, spiders, and rats feeding on each other, and sometimes on us! We lost a lot of weight. But we did have our brains, our bodies, and our hearts, and that was enough.

Never underestimate the power of the human spirit.

Prior to 1970, activities that would strengthen your mind or body, such as making or using a homemade deck of cards or exercising would win you a trip to the torture chamber. It was during this long, dark night of terror that Dick Nixon won the 1968 presidential election. I was convinced this war hawk would end the Vietnam conflict soon, so it was time to get in shape. I asked myself, "How do I become fit without resorting to traditional, mind-numbing, boring exercises?" I told a POW friend my workout routine would have to be fun—something I had never done or seen anyone else do. I concluded that one-hand handstands with either hand would be a great choice.

It took me two years to master that skill with either hand. I wouldn't have been able to do so if I had not been so passionately committed to learning how to do it, which I was.

I've often said, "If you are trying to accomplish a difficult task without passion and you are smacked in the face, you will fold up like a cheap accordion. On the other hand, if you are passionate about the endeavor, you will get pissed. Passion gives you the strength to endure the pain to be successful."

Find a reason to be passionate, and success will follow.

One-Handed Handstands, Juggling, and Banana Whiskey

I arrived in the Hanoi Hilton able to do a two-hand handstand.

My first attempt at a one-hand handstand revealed that my arm was locked in the shoulder socket. I did not have the strength to support my body weight and extend my arm out of my shoulder socket at the same time. Only my wrist was available for balance.

I quickly discovered that to do a one-hand handstand, you must have the strength to support your body weight while your arm is extended out of your shoulder socket. This allows your arm to move in any direction to maintain balance. Your wrist is also a factor in maintaining balance but can make only small corrections.

The torture I had endured pulled my shoulders out of the sockets, ripping tendons and subjecting that area of my body to severe and lasting trauma. My first reaction was to say to myself, "What the heck am I going to do now?

I decided I would start doing handstand push-ups to strengthen my shoulders. Starting in a two-hand handstand, I would lower myself all the way down, touch my nose to the ground, and push myself all the way back up. I was lifting my entire body weight up and down. It took one year for my shoulders to become strong enough for me to do unaided sets of fifty handstand push-ups at a time. By that time, extending my arm out of the shoulder socket was no problem. So now it was time to practice one-hand handstands with either hand.

My practice routine was to place a bucket upside down on the floor and put a folded blanket on top to adjust the height. Placing my right hand on the floor and my left hand on the blanket, I would kick up into a two-hand handstand. I would then slowly transfer all my weight to my right hand as I extended my arm out of the socket. It took me one more year to master a one-hand handstand using my right hand. With practice, I could jump into the air and land on my right hand while holding my legs together, straight up in the air, while balancing on one hand. I could stay there for about a minute. It took less than a month to accomplish the same task with my left hand.

In these photos, I demonstrate my famous one-hand handstand. These photos were taken after I returned from the war. My shoulders were misaligned after the torture I endured.

Then I started juggling. Usually, I juggled five balls in the air, and I eventually got up to six balls. You have to throw them higher when you have that many. The balls were all different sizes and shapes because they were made of whatever I could find, and it was a mess trying to catch them. They ended up going all over the place. Meanwhile, my other buddies were learning languages and doing other things that challenged their minds and bodies.

As an example, a buddy of mine whom we called King Dog helped me make booze. We found a crock pot made of clay. At that time in our captivity, the Vietnamese were giving us bananas to eat. King Dog and I grabbed all the banana peelings we could find. We put them in a crock pot to make whiskey. I got up one night and saw that fermentation had pushed the lid off the pot. I awakened King Dog, who helped me pour all the booze into another container. We then awakened our fellow POWs and treated each of them to a shot of banana whiskey. That was an unforgettable event. Mostly, we were helping each other stay out of trouble and supporting those who were in pain and suffering. It wasn't like we didn't have plenty to do.

Juggling five balls.

After Ho's death, by 1970, classical torture, the breaking of bones, the ripping of flesh, and beatings with a rubber hose had ended. At that point, it was just harassment, isolation, and beatings. For the first time, we had an opportunity to take our brains and start thinking of things besides survival. The end to torture had an indescribable and profoundly positive impact on our physical and mental well-being. Our individual and collective achievements speak for themselves. In the physical arena, the winner of our camp-wide push-up contest posted 606 push-ups without stopping. The sit-up contest winner posted more than 5,000 sit-ups nonstop, and I learned how to juggle five homemade balls and do one-hand handstands with either hand.

Weighing Ourselves in a Cistern

In the mental realm, our achievements were also remarkable. Over time, we developed the skill to resolve complex computations with our brains alone. You can accomplish this in your head, but not right away. You have to spend about a thousand hours or so before you can become good at it, and we had plenty of hours to work on problems. In other words, your brain becomes your personal computer. You learn how to create a file, solve a problem, edit results, and save the solution, every detail captured in your God-given, magnificent brain.

For example, using the binomial theorem $(A+B)^N$, we were able to derive compound-interest formulas for any set of conditions you could imagine—for example, investing a lump sum compounded annually or investing quarterly compound daily. Our challenge was to carry all the calculations essential to deriving a correct compound interest formula in our heads. That was tricky to do because some of those lines of calculations, if written down, would be three feet wide.

The value of knowledge was illustrated when one of my fellow POWs came up with a way to weigh ourselves. In front of our cellblock, we had a courtyard. In it was a cistern. It was made of brick and mortar and stood four foot high. The opening at the top was 3 ft. by 3 ft. and was symmetrical. We could fill it with water and wash clothes.

One sweltering-hot July day, we sat staring at that cistern, and a POW buddy came up with an idea. We stole a ruler from one of the interrogation rooms. We found a stick, and using the ruler, we marked it off in metric units. We replaced the ruler to avoid detection.

We filled the cistern with water until it was running out the top. A POW stepped into the top of the water column and submerged. When the water quit running out, someone tapped him on the head. As he was stepping out of the cistern, brushing off the remaining water droplets into the tank, the door to our courtyard opened. In came the camp commander and a bunch of guards. They were all excited. The camp commander pointed at him and yelled, "What on earth are you Americans up to?"

The POW looked at the camp commander and said, "We are weighing ourselves." The camp commander immediately adopted an inscrutable, confused look and said, "How can you do this?"

My POW friend responded, "Archimedes."

A confused camp commander then asked, "Who is this Archimedes?"

My friend responded, "I don't think I'm going to be able to 'splain it to you."

About that time, another POW came running up with that stick. He stuck it in the tank and measured the linear displacement of the water. He dropped down on one knee, grabbed a rock, and started scribbling on the ground. He looked up at his wet POW buddy and said, "One hundred fourteen."

At that point, the senior ranking officer of the cellblock said to the camp commander, "Look at us. When we were shot down, we weighed 170, 160, 150 US pounds. Now my fellow POW weighs 114 US pounds. We need food."

The camp commander then adopted a look of understanding and said, "Yes, I guess he weighs 114 US pounds. How did you do that?"

Archimedes' principle says a body immersed in a fluid is buoyed up with a force equal to the weight of the fluid displaced by the body. Take a ship that weighs 10,000 pounds and place it on the surface of a smooth lake. As it sinks into the lake, its hull displaces water. When it has displaced its weight in water it stabilizes, or it's going to go to the bottom of the sea. You can measure your weight within a pound or so.

That is what we did. We were doing all kinds of experiments with our minds, in ways that we could not replicate today.

Never underestimate the value of knowledge.

Chapter 11

LEARN PATIENCE AS A POWERFUL TOOL FOR SUCCESS

Jim

Imagine having to wait a long period of time to gain your freedom. At times, it will seem hopeless, and it will be tempting to give up. No one would blame you if you did. But for those who have the resilience to persevere, freedom is possible.

Barry and his fellow POWs did not know if they would ever get to go home. But just in case they did get to, they prepared themselves for that blessed day by keeping busy, physically fit, and expanding their minds. Despair was not in their vocabulary. They trusted that they would be released—and they were.

We can all learn an important life lesson from Barry's story. Patience is a powerful tool for both survival and success.

Barry
In the spring of 1970, we became convinced that the government of North Vietnam had decided to stop the torture program.

Bill Baugh Tortured to Sign for a Package

One of the North Vietnamese guards' last attempts to inflict systematic torture on the American POWs was demanding a confession before a POW could receive a package from home.

For the first time, a fellow POW—Bill Baugh, now deceased—was taken to a meeting to receive a package from home. We celebrated, but too soon. It was two days later that our POW friend returned.

We asked, "Where have you been?"

He said, "In the torture chamber."

We asked, "What the heck was that all about?"

He responded, "They wanted me to sign a receipt for my package."

He displayed a small package in his hand. I said, "Well, why didn't you sign the damn receipt?"

He responded, "You need to read what the receipt said."

It read, "I want to thank the lenient people of North Vietnam for allowing me to have a package from my home, even though I was a participant in killing thousands of Vietnamese by bombing the dams and dike systems of North Vietnam, denying them food and shelter."

It was a propaganda statement. He said, "I told them, 'I'm not going to sign that damn thing for some cheese crackers. You've got to be kidding me.' So they tortured me for two days to sign the damn receipt."

The torture chamber was clearly still alive and well. When the rest of us learned that a POW had been tortured to sign a propaganda receipt to receive a package from home, we informed the North Vietnamese camp authority that the guards could have our cheese crackers. Our unified action ultimately forced the camp authority to cancel the package-receipt requirement.

A Good-Guy Camp—Camp Faith

In the summer of 1970, the camp authority moved approximately 250 American POWs into a new prison camp we named Camp Faith. The prison compound was split evenly into two sections by a high concrete wall. Each side would hold 125 POWs. It became clear early on that the camp authority had been ordered to house us, feed us, give us our packages, and leave us alone. We were interned in large rooms with liberal access to a large courtyard, where we could exercise and sun ourselves.

The Son Tay Raid

We were in Camp Faith for about six months when late one night, chaos ensued. In the middle of the night, helicopters hovered overhead. We heard sonic booms, SAM missiles going off, and bombs exploding. The place was bedlam. Two days later, we figured out that the United States had launched a rescue attempt for American Vietnam POWs code-named the "Son Tay Raid."

The Son Tay Raid was designed to rescue American POWs. Our Air Force and other intelligence sources suggested there were about fifty American POWs in a prison camp we called Camp Hope. As the crow flies, it was a few miles away from the prison camp we were in. What our intelligence services did not understand was that their information was faulty. There was nobody in Camp Hope except a bunch of Chinese regular soldiers, all of whom were killed by the American raiding party. They found no POWs. So they boarded their helicopters and flew out of there, unsuccessful.

At that time, the North Vietnamese were also scared to death that another raid might be eminent for another of their many isolated American POW camps. Within one day, they relocated all American POWs from outlying prisons to the central prison of Hỏa Lò, downtown Hanoi that allowed the North Vietnamese Government to incarcerate our POWs into a few large prisons rather than a lot of small ones. This approach made it easier to guard against rescue by US Special Forces. The bad news of Son Tay was a failure to rescue American POWs. The good news was, the forced consolidation strengthened our capacity to organize, resist, and survive.

The Son Tay Raid Sends a Stark Warning to the North Vietnamese[29]

A combined US Air Force and US Army team of forty Americans led by Army Colonel "Bull" Simons conducted a raid on the Son Tay prison camp, twenty-three miles west of Hanoi, to free between seventy and one hundred Americans suspected of being held there.

Planning for the mission—code-named Operation Ivory Coast—began in June 1970. The plan called for US Army Special Forces (Green Berets) to be flown to Son Tay by helicopter and crash-land inside the compound. The plan was for one group of Green Berets to pour out of the helicopter and neutralize any opposition while Green Berets in other helicopters, landing outside the walls, would break in and complete the rescue operation.

At 11:30 p.m. on November 20, the raiding force departed Takhli Royal Thai Air Force Base in Thailand. As the force approached the camp, US Air Force and Navy warplanes struck North Vietnamese troop installations and antiaircraft sites in the area. Part of the force initially landed at the wrong compound, but otherwise the mission came off without a hitch.

Unfortunately, the Green Berets could not locate any prisoners in the huts. After a sharp firefight with the North Vietnamese troops in the area, the order was given to withdraw, and twenty-seven minutes after the raid began, the force was in the air, headed back to Thailand. The raid was accomplished in a superb manner, and all Americans returned safely, but it was learned later that the prisoners had been moved elsewhere in July. Despite that disappointment, the raid was a tactical success and sent a message to the North Vietnamese that the United States could insert an undetected combat force only miles from their capital.

Stunned by the raid, high-ranking Hanoi officials ordered all US POWs moved to several central prison complexes. This was actually a welcome change the move afforded the prisoners more contact with each other and boosted their morale.

Determined to Practice Our Faith in Hoa Lò Prison

In the spring of 1971, in the central prison of Hỏa Lò, approximately 250 American POWs, in open defiance of the camp authority, began to conduct church services, share Scriptures, and sing religious and patriotic songs at the

---

29 "This Day in History: November 21, 1970—US Force Raids Son Tay Prison Camp," History. com, https://www.history.com/this-day-in-history/u-s-force-raids-son-tay-prison-camp.

top of our lungs. If you had been in Hanoi on that faithful day, you would have heard those songs reverberating off the buildings in the downtown part of the city. True to form, in the wee hours of morning that followed, in came the storm troopers to crush the religious and patriotic rebellion. They identified thirty-six American POWs they considered to be troublemakers and instigators. I was one of the instigators.

They put us in trucks, took us across the city, and dropped us into a punishment camp consisting of thirty-six individual solitary confinement cells. They were sending a message to the men back at the central prison that if you don't cease and desist this religious and patriotic revolt, you will receive some of the same. But on this occasion, the men back at the central prison put their heads together and said, "You know, it's been a while since we've been engaged in a mass torture session, so why don't we push our limits to test them?"

The men kept on conducting church services, sharing Scripture, and singing religious and patriotic songs. The government of North Vietnam had a decision to make, and they did. After all those years of horror, they ordered the camp authority to stand down. We had finally won the right to openly worship in our rooms, which, as you can imagine, became an immediate source of strength and a unifying factor.

While we were there, one night, out of nowhere, the door to my cell opened. The guard shoved Orson Swindle, a POW buddy of mine, into my room and shut the door. Nobody wanted to room with Orson because he was always going to the torture chamber, and if you were his roommate, you have to go, too.

I said, "Orson, what the heck are you doing in my room?"

He replied, "I get to be your roommate."

I said, "Orson, there's two things you need to understand. Number one, you deserve to be in this punishment camp. And number two, you darn sure don't need to be my roommate."

Skid Row

The arrival of the thirty-six troublemakers at the Skid Row prison was foreboding! The camp authority's solution to overcome any resistance by American POWs was always immediate and brutal torture. We had good reason to believe the camp authority was now convinced that the strength of America's Vietnam POWs to resist exploitation rested in the hands of the few, who could be identified, isolated, and broken. We were the guinea pigs.

But what the Vietnamese did not understand was that the willingness of America's warriors to resist exploitation is not determined by the strength of the few but by the values our warriors hold in common. Over time, it became clear to Skid Row prisoners that our fears of torture to confront resistance by American POWs had been replaced by a new policy of banishment for POWs who did not cooperate with the North Vietnamese camp authority.

We were in exile for about a year before rejoining our fellow POWs in the central prison of Hỏa Lò in August 1971.

May 1972: Dog Patch Camp Opens

In May 1972, in the wee hours of the morning, the North Vietnamese camp authority trucked 220 healthy American POWs to a Chinese highway checkpoint. Chinese soldiers authorized our truck convoy entry and use of the road, which continued straight north. Seventy miles later, the convoy turned west and re-entered North Vietnam. Shortly thereafter, we passed through a gate into a prison camp with a lot of small buildings on the side of a hill surrounded by a fence. We named the camp "Dog Patch."

Healthy American POWs who required minimal medical care and who could be easily moved into China provided Hanoi with a potentially powerful bargaining chip to complicate future US Special Forces rescue efforts. We were interned into buildings that would hold eight to ten POWs. They fed us and left us alone.

An Unwelcome Visit from Hanoi Jane

One day, the door opened, and in walked the camp commander. He was carrying a recorder. The guards gathered all the POWs into one room to hear a recorded message. The commander introduced the recording with, "Today, I allow you to hear from a great American."

All of us were thinking, "Yeah, I'll bet."

In walked actress Jane Fonda.

What Hanoi Jane Said Back in 1972[30]

According to History News Network, when Jane Fonda arrived in Hanoi on July 8, 1972, she told her welcoming hosts that she carried with her "greetings" from revolutionary "comrades" in America. She was there, willingly and knowingly, "to provide grist for the North Vietnamese propaganda mill."

She made nineteen speeches over Radio Hanoi. In one of them, Fonda commented on her recent meeting with seven "US aggressor pilots." She said she had found them "healthy and repentant." She also said of the meeting, "We had a very long talk, a very open and casual talk. We exchanged ideas freely. They asked me to bring back to the American people their sense of disgust of the war and their shame for what they have been asked to do." According to Fonda, the pilots requested that she encourage their "loved ones and friends…to please be as actively involved in the peace movement as possible."

In fact, the pilots with whom Fonda met were neither healthy nor repentant. Nor had they been at liberty to engage in conversation with the starlet.

When Fonda started speaking, about five of us abruptly stood up and started for the door. Standing in the doorway was a guard we called Dink. He was 4'8". He had a rifle with a bayonet that reached three feet over his head. He would've made a great recruiting poster to join the North Vietnamese Army. He was hilarious. We could see Dink's beady little eyes looking at us from underneath his pit helmet. They were getting bigger and bigger as we walked toward him. Dink started banging the butt of his gun on the concrete floor. *Bang, bang!*

I said, "Dink, get out of the way. We're coming through, buddy." And like a tsunami, we moved him out of the way, exited through the doorway, and down the hall we went. We knew there could be consequences, but we were willing to take the risk.

Two POWs stayed behind and listened to the rest of the story. I can forgive Jane Fonda for her uninformed and hurtful comments, but her image on an

---

30   Edward J. Renehan, Jr., "Lest We Forget: The Case against Jane Fonda," History News Network, Columbian College of Arts & Sciences at The George Washington University, https://historynewsnetwork.org/article/1050.

anti-aircraft gun will live in infamy. However, Attorney General Ramsey Clark was really duped.

Ramsey Clark, following his term as the attorney general during the administration of Lyndon B. Johnson, worked as a law professor and was active in the anti-Vietnam War movement.[31] He interviewed POWs during a trip to Vietnam and said they were "unquestionably...well treated." Since the 1970s, Clark opposed US military interventions wherever they occurred, including Vietnam.

Like Jane Fonda, Clark was concerned about dikes being destroyed in non-military areas. He was pictured in a photograph standing on a dike in North Vietnam with a two-thousand-pound bomb lying on top of the dike. Later, a congressional panel interrogated Clark. A panel member asked him, "How do you get a two-thousand-pound bomb to lie down on a soft-sod dike? How did that happen?"

I can tell you how: the Vietnamese carried it up there and set it on the dang dike. If a 2,000-pound bomb had been dropped on the dike, it would be at least twenty-five feet below the surface, or it would have exploded.

I can't forgive him for being so stupid. He knew better, but the Vietnamese used him, big time.

Operation Linebacker: President Nixon Sends in the B-52s

While we were in the Dog Patch prison camp, the next big event that occurred was Dick Nixon launching Operation Linebacker II. The President decided he'd had enough. The peace talks weren't going anywhere, so he sent in the B-52 bombers to attack strategic targets in the Hanoi area in a campaign called Linebacker II.

The US used B-52s along the DMZ to carpet-bomb truck traffic and North Vietnamese soldiers trying to infiltrate into South Vietnam. This was the first time B-52s were used to attack high-value targets in and around the Hanoi area. The bombardment lasted twelve days, with a loss of sixteen B-52s.

---

31 "Ramsey Clark," The United States Department of Justice, https://www.justice.gov/enrd/ramsey-clark.

At that point, the North Vietnamese had no more SA-2 missiles, which was the most effective weapon against the high-flying B-52s. It was now, "Katie bar the door." A large number of my POWs friends were in the Hanoi area throughout the bombardment. They lamented to me later, "You missed the greatest show on Earth."

Communication between buildings in the Dog Patch prison camp was accomplished almost exclusively with the POW hand code and great eyes. In those days, you had to have great health, especially great eyesight, to become a pilot. Most of us had 20/20 vision, and some of us had 20/10. Great eyes allowed us to read code off each other's fingers and communicate, even though our buildings were 50 to 100 yards apart.

One day while I was engaged in routine communication with another building, I was informed that a guard had told the men in his room that two B-52s had been shot down the over Hanoi. My note-taker and I were in disbelief. I requested and received a confirmation from the other building. I then turned to the POW I was working with and said, "If true, do you know what this means?"

He said, "Make it good."

I responded, "It means we're going home. Dick Nixon would not send the B-52s to the Hanoi area without every intention of sending in the 82nd Airborne behind them, if that's what it takes. This war is going to end."

It did, within weeks.

On January 27, 1973, the Paris Peace Accords were signed, officially ending the American war in Vietnam. One of the prerequisites for and provisions of the accords was the return of all US prisoners of war. My fellow POWs and I departed Dog Patch Prison Camp on January 31, 1973, and relocated to Hỏa Lò prison, pending repatriation. Senior American Vietnam POW leadership established a code for release. Sick and wounded would go first. POWs would not accept early release. They would return home only in the order they were shot down and captured.

Secretary of State Henry Kissinger was in Hanoi for the second round, in which 112 POWs would be sent home. As a sign of goodwill, the North Vietnamese Government asked him to select an additional twenty men to be released. Unaware of the POW repatriation code, he circled twenty names at random. The men he selected refused to violate the POW release code. It took five days; a direct order from USAF Col. Gaddis, the senior American officer, and POWs left at the Hanoi Hilton; and the stipulation of no photographs of them to gain cooperation.

Operation Linebacker II Leads to the End of the Vietnam War[32]

In the winter of 1972, the Nixon administration announced that the bombing and mining of North Vietnam would resume and continue until a "settlement" was reached. On December 13, North Vietnamese negotiators walked out of secret talks with National Security Advisor Henry Kissinger.

President Richard Nixon issued an ultimatum to Hanoi to send its representatives back to the conference table within 72 hours, "or else." The North Vietnamese rejected Nixon's demand, and the president ordered Operation Linebacker II, a full-scale air campaign against the Hanoi area. White House Press Secretary Ronald Ziegler said that the bombing would end only if all US prisoners of war were released and an internationally recognized cease-fire was in force.

Linebacker II was the most concentrated air offensive of the war. It was conducted by US aircraft, including B-52s, US Air Force fighter-bombers flying from bases in Thailand, and Navy and Marine fighter-bombers flying from carriers in the South China Sea. During the 11 days of the attack, 700 B-52 sorties and more than 1,000 fighter-bomber sorties were flown. These planes dropped roughly 20,000 tons of bombs, mostly over the densely populated area between Hanoi and Haiphong.

The North Vietnamese fired more than 1,000 surface-to-air missiles at the attacking aircraft and used their MiG fighter-interceptor squadrons, eight of which were shot down. In a throwback to past aerial combat, Staff Sgt. Samuel O. Turner, the tail gunner on a Boeing B-52D bomber, downed a trailing MiG-21 with a blast from his .50 caliber machine guns over Hanoi. Six days later, Airman First Class Albert E. Moore, also a B-52 gunner, shot down a second MiG-21 after a strike on the Thai Nguyen rail yard. These were the only aerial gunner kills of the war. Twenty-six US aircraft were lost, including 15 B-52s. Three

---

32   "This Day in History: December 18, 1972—Nixon Orders the Initiation of Operation Linebacker II," History.com, https://www.history.com/this-day-in-history/nixon-orders-the-initiation-of-operation-linebacker-ii.

aircraft were brought down by MiG's; the rest, including the B-52s, were downed by surface-to-air missiles.

The Linebacker II bombing was deemed a success because in its wake, the North Vietnamese returned to the negotiating table, where the Paris Peace Accords were signed less than a month later.

Back in Hanoi, I was waiting. For the first time, we were able to mingle with each other a little bit. I got to talk to Vice Admiral James Stockdale and Colonel Robbie Reisner, who are both deceased now, but never forgotten. They were wonderful human beings—the kind of folks who understood the importance of values, character, and confidence. These are the kind of people who surrounded me.

In my opinion, the late Vice Admiral James B. Stockdale was one of the most extraordinary, exemplary leaders we had in North Vietnam.

Vice Admiral James B. Stockdale: An Extraordinary Hero[33]

On September 9, 1965, at the age of forty-one, Vice Admiral James B. Stockdale, at that time a US Navy Commander, VF51 and Carrier Air Group Commander (CAG-16), was catapulted from the deck of the *USS Oriskany* for what would be the final mission. While returning from the target area, his A-4 Skyhawk was hit by anti-aircraft fire. Stockdale ejected, breaking a bone in his back. Upon landing in a small village, he badly dislocated his knee, which subsequently went untreated and eventually left him with a fused knee joint and a very distinctive gait.

Stockdale wound up in Hỏa Lò Prison, the infamous "Hanoi Hilton," where he spent the next seven years as the highest-ranking naval officer and leader of American resistance against Vietnamese attempts to use prisoners for propaganda purposes. Despite being kept in solitary confinement for four years, in leg irons for two years, physically tortured more than fifteen times, denied medical care, and malnourished, Stockdale organized a system of communication and developed a cohesive set of rules governing prisoner behavior. Codified in the acronym BACK U.S. (Unity over Self), these rules gave prisoners a sense of

---

33   "Vice Admiral James B. Stockdale," United States Naval Academy, https://www.usna.edu/Ethics/bios/stockdale.php.

hope and empowerment. Many of the prisoners credited these rules as giving them the strength to endure their lengthy ordeal. Drawing largely from principles of stoic philosophy, notably Epictetus's The Enchiridion, Stockdale's courage and decisive leadership were an inspiration to POWs.

The climax of the struggle of wills between American POWs and their captors came in the spring of 1969. Told he was to be taken "downtown" and paraded in front of foreign journalists, Stockdale slashed his scalp with a razor and beat himself in the face with a wooden stool, knowing that his captors would not display a prisoner who was disfigured. Later, after discovering that some prisoners had died during torture, he slashed his wrists to demonstrate to his captors that he preferred death to submission. This act so convinced the Vietnamese of his determination to die rather than to cooperate that the Communists ceased the torture of American prisoners and gradually improved their treatment of POWs. Upon his release from prison in 1973, Stockdale's extraordinary heroism became widely known, and President Gerald Ford awarded him The Medal of Honor in 1976.

He was one of the most highly decorated officers in the history of the Navy, wearing twenty-six personal combat decorations, including two Distinguished Flying Crosses, three Distinguished Service Medals, two Purple Hearts, and four Silver Star medals in addition to the Medal of Honor. He was the only three-star admiral in the history of the Navy to wear both aviator wings and the Medal of Honor.

When asked what experiences he thought were essential to his survival and ultimate success in the prison, Admiral Stockdale referred to events early in his life: his childhood experiences in his mother's local drama productions, which encouraged spontaneity, humor, and theatrical timing; the lessons of how to endure physical pain as a football player in high school and college; and his determination to live up to the promise he made to his father upon entering the Naval Academy that he would be the best midshipmen he could be. It was the uniquely American ability to improvise in tight situations, Stockdale believed, that gave him the confidence that the POWs could outwit their captors and return home with honor, despite their dire situation.

On the Way Home—Sick but Free

When I boarded the United States C-141 aircraft to leave North Vietnam, I had pneumonia and a temperature of 104 degrees. I was sick as a dog but didn't feel it. There were about one hundred POWs on our aircraft, but you could have heard a pin drop as we taxied out to take off. Our silence continued as we left North Vietnamese airspace and headed out over the Gulf of Tokin.

We all knew our aircraft could still be shot down by their air defense systems until we were well off the coast of North Vietnam. So we just sat quietly, waiting, listening for the crack of the mic button to signal we were safe. When we heard the click, it was followed by the words, "Let's party!"

The place went bonkers.

First Stop: The Philippines

America's Vietnam POWs released from North Vietnam were flown into the Philippine Islands for initial medical care and debriefings. Some POWs had serious medical issues that needed immediate attention. For others, changes in the family structure required sensitive and careful discussions with the military member. Once cleared to go home, we were assigned by our respective military services to a military base that could provide the support we needed as close as possible to our homes.

The Paris Peace Accords End the American War in Vietnam[34]

On January 27, 1973, the Paris Peace Accords were signed, officially ending the American war in Vietnam. One of the prerequisites for and provisions of the accords was the return of all US prisoners of war (POWs).

On February 12, the first of 591 U.S. military and civilian POWs were released in Hanoi and flown directly to Clark Air Force Base in the Philippines. A year later, in the State of the Union address, President Richard M. Nixon told the American people, "All our troops have returned from Southeast Asia—and they have returned with honor."

Yet many Americans were starting to question whether all POWs had been released. The Vietnam POW issue became a major controversy, prompting congressional investigations, partisan politics, the production of major motion pictures (e.g., *Uncommon Valor* in 1983 and *Rambo: First Blood Part II* in 1985), and the formation of a number of POW organizations, such as the National League of POW/MIA Families.

---

34   Adrian R. Lewis, "Vietnam War POWs and MIAs," *Encyclopaedia Britannica*, https://www.britannica.com/topic/Vietnam-War-POWs-and-MIAs-2051428.

In a poll by *The Wall Street Journal* and NBC News in 1991, 69 percent of the American people believed that US POWs were still being held in Indochina, and 52 percent had concluded that the government was derelict in not securing their release. The uproar over POWs caused the Senate to form the Select Committee on POW/MIA Affairs, chaired by Democrat John Kerry and including several other veterans of the war, among them Republican John McCain. The controversy was fed by reported live sightings and photographs of Americans held in captivity. Investigations revealed that the photographs were phony, and the sightings could not be verified. Indeed, no credible evidence was ever provided to substantiate the claim that American POWs continued to languish in Vietnam after the signing of the peace accords. Nevertheless, the POW issue remained significant.

The Vietnam POW/MIA issue is unique for several reasons. The Vietnam War was the first war the United States lost. Consequently, after the war it was impossible for the United States to search the battlefields for remains of its dead and missing. Because North Vietnam was never occupied, it was impossible to search prisons and cemeteries there. In addition, North Vietnam shared a common border with the People's Republic of China, and it had close ties with the Soviet Union; unknown numbers of POWs may have been taken to both of those countries. Finally, much of Vietnam is covered with dense jungle; the geography, terrain, and climate make it exceedingly difficult to find and recover remains. All those factors damaged recovery efforts and precluded a comprehensive, accurate accounting. Nevertheless, on July 11, 1995, the United States extended diplomatic recognition to Vietnam—an act that gave Americans greater access to the country.

In 1973, when the POWs were released, roughly 2,500 servicemen were designated "missing in action" (MIA). As of 2015, more than 1,600 of those were still "unaccounted for." The Defense POW/MIA Accounting Agency (DPAA) of the US Department of Defense lists 687 US POWs as having returned alive from the Vietnam War. North Vietnam acknowledged that 55 American servicemen and 7 civilians died in captivity. During the war, POWs in Hanoi prisons endeavored to maintain a registry of captive Americans; they concluded that at least 766 POWs entered the system. POWs were initially held in four prisons in Hanoi and six facilities within 50 miles of the city.

More than 80 percent of POWs held in North Vietnam were aircrew personnel of the US Air Force (332 POWs), US Navy (149 POWs), and US Marine Corps (28 POWs). POWs held in North Vietnam were used for propaganda, psychological warfare, and negotiating purposes. They were tortured, isolated, and psychologically abused in violation of the Geneva Convention of 1949, to which North Vietnam was a signatory.

Chapter 12

ADAPT AS YOUR LIFE CHANGES

Jim

During the COVID-19 pandemic of 2020, I read about people who had gone "off the grid" for a year or so, returning home to discover everyone trying to survive the fast-spreading pandemic. They describe how surreal it was to envision returning home to the life they had known, only to find something much different awaiting them.

That's exactly what happened to Barry. When he finally returned home, he discovered that the world had changed. So he adapted.

This is one of the most important lessons in life, relationships, and business: we must adapt as our lives change, or we will be miserable, always fighting reality and wishing for "the way things were."

Barry
An Antipatriotic Sentiment in America

When we returned home, America's Vietnam POWs did not receive the backlash that other Vietnam War Veterans experienced when they returned home from Vietnam. But because we were cut off from any news, we did not know that veterans had experienced such hatred from some of the American public until we returned.

Our Vietnam War veterans were asked to do the impossible: win a land war on the continent of Asia. Their reward for that Herculean bloody endeavor was a silent and sometimes hostile homecoming - a despicable chapter in American history that will forever remain in the halls of infamy.

Now, that's the bad news. The good news is, America's Vietnam War veterans were not a bunch of wimps. They came home with honor, held no grudge, and went back to work. They are a national treasure, the guarantors of our liberty.

Jim

About the time the POWs were preparing to return in 1972, it was announced that I was going to the US Naval Academy. There was a certain group of people in my high school who thought that going into the military was one of the worst things one could possibly do because of the Vietnam War.

At the Naval Academy, the younger students went to class six days a week. They had Saturday afternoons off and could go into town. Sometimes, we could go at night. The Naval Academy is right next to St. John's University, which is a liberal arts university. Sometimes midshipmen were jeered, spat upon, had empty beer bottles thrown at them, and sometimes had trash dumped on them. This was particularly bad during the warm months, when we wore white uniforms. I had such deep respect for our military during that time because I didn't serve in Vietnam; I attended college at the end of the war. Our Vietnam veterans were not treated well.

Barry
Finally, My First Drink of Real Alcohol

When I arrived back home, my brother and everybody in the town was at our house. My brother, McRae, said, "Barry, please have a drink with me. You've never had a drink." So I had my first drink of alcohol ever with my brother (the banana whiskey in Hanoi didn't count). I wanted him to know I cared enough about him to have a drink with him. That's when I started drinking occasionally. Today, sometimes I'll drink a glass of wine or two in the evening.

What a blessed occasion I thought I'd never live to see—reuniting with my family.

I was thrilled to ride through my beloved hometown of Bladenboro, North Carolina, again—a free man after six and a half years as a POW in the Hanoi Hilton.

This is my favorite photo—at my homecoming parade, with the glorious American flag in the foreground. The American flag deserves our utmost respect because it symbolizes the precious, hard-won freedom we enjoy as a sovereign nation.

My Greatest Disappointment: The American News Media

People have asked me, "What was your biggest disappointment when you came home?"

My answer is always, "The lack of a news media that I could trust." If the media is truly busting its rear ends to understand what's going on and is reporting the news honestly and sincerely, our nation will flourish. When it is not, we are in trouble.

The news media were a huge disappointment to me because of the way they interacted with me as a POW coming out of Hanoi and the way they still conduct themselves. Within two weeks of the time I walked out of Hanoi, I was in my hometown, walking into my front door. The phone rang, and a lady from *Meet the Press* was on the line. She said, "Captain Bridger, we'd like to fly you to New York and be on *Meet the Press* this Sunday as our guest."

My response was, "Why? Why me?"

She said, "Well, all the POWs you know are coming home, and American people want to know what happened."

I immediately bristled when I heard her remarks. At that time, there were still American POWs waiting to be released.

I said to her, "Ma'am, are you aware that all of the American POWs are not out of Hanoi?"

She said, "Yes, but the American people deserve to know what happened."

I was astounded. I took a deep breath of air and said, "Ma'am, are you listening carefully?" I was trying not to be rude.

She responded, "Well, yeah."

I said, "The American people don't give a ding-dang what happened until they get their people home. Are you out of your mind? No!"

I hung the phone up and said, "What the heck was that all about? Surely that lady wasn't from *Meet the Press*."

Within about two weeks, the phone rang again. Same lady, same request, same response from me. She said, "Well, all the prisoners are out of Hanoi."

I replied, "How do you know that?"

There was a pause, and then she said, "Well, I read it in the paper."

I said, "Ma'am, do you believe that there are mothers, fathers, brothers, and sisters who are waiting and praying that their loved ones are still going to come home? Do these American neighbors deserve our empathy, or should we just write them off and start talking?"

She said, "Well—"

I cut her off and said with great emotion, "Ma'am, I am not about to participate in that. We owe more to our fellow Americans who are still praying for their loved ones to get off an aircraft. No! Bye."

Some of my POW buddies decided to go on that program, and that disappointed me. I never watched the program, and I would never go on it. I was amazed that a responsible adult in our country would suggest we talk publicly about our experiences while some of our warriors were still in North Vietnam. I saw it as a chance for the TV stations to acquire ratings, with insufficient concern about the possible consequences.

There is a tremendous amount of inaccurate reporting of the news today. This is not good for America because the news should inform and unite us, not divide us. Americans should be able to make their own decisions rather than be told what to think by news correspondents. Report the facts, and let the American public figure it out. I personally have no doubt that if we had honorable, independent, no-nonsense news media that pursued the facts relentlessly and with empathy, our divided nation would come together like the speed of heat.

Presidents come and go. The voting public and the Constitution provide the exit. Big media are much more difficult to control. But there is an exit. I quit listening and watching. It quickly dawned on me that I could not trust networks, but I could trust individuals because there were still people in the news business when I came home whom I could not co-opt. Among my trusted reporters then were Howard K. Smith, David Brinkley, and Chet Huntley. They were serious, professional, honorable reporters who understood the power of traditional American values, and an honest news media, and shared them with the public.

Our media are not so serious about reporting the facts today. It seems to me that they are all political and unreliable.

In some countries, such as what we experienced in Vietnam, China, and North Korea, what do the leaders take over first when they are trying to control the people? They take over the media, and they tell the news media what to say. Unlike in the United States, those citizens cannot speak freely. We face similar problems when our news media tell us what to think and rile up the masses over insignificant and unreliable reporting.

Bumping into John McCain Again

When John McCain became the Republican nominee for president of the United States in the 2008 election, he traveled to Kansas City, and I went to the rally. He didn't know I was there. I was just standing in the audience. At the end of the presentation, he walked around the stage shaking hands with everybody. He was with his running mate, Sarah Palin, and her husband.

McCain came up to me, and I reached out to shake his hand. All the bright lights and the swarm of people momentarily blinded him. He didn't know it was me standing there. Finally, I grabbed him by the shoulders and shook him. I said, "John, it's Bridger."

He looked at me, and suddenly, he recognized me. He said, "Barry?"

I said, "Yes." Then I said, "How can I help you besides sending you some silly money?"

"Boy, I really need some help," he said.

I said, "Well, you realize, of course, that Paul the Apostle could not win this election."

He got a funny look on his face.

I said, "But you have an advantage."

"Well," he said, "what's that?"

I said, "Well, if I recall correctly, they took Paul's head off. You'll be OK."

McCain said, "Contact my people in Washington. I need help—lots of it."

So I contacted one of his handlers. He was aware that I was going to call him, and he asked me to go to Philadelphia to be a guest speaker at the 150th birthday ball for the Republican Party. I put together a presentation, and I went to Philadelphia to deliver the speech. But McCain wasn't there. Tom Ridge, who is a former governor of Pennsylvania, a former member of the US House of Representatives, and the first US Secretary of Homeland Security from 2003 to 2005, was at my table.

When all 525 of us POWs finally got home, we scattered like a cubby of quail. Everybody disappeared into a big world, and we all began our new lives. A lot of POWs went to regular POW meetings. I didn't because I was dating, getting married, and having children, the things a lot of Vietnam POWs had already done. I had more important things to do than go eat mashed potatoes and hamburgers, or whatever they had.

Sometimes, Experience Trumps Education

In his best-selling book *Outliers*, English author Malcolm Gladwell shares with us that success is not about smarts but discovering and developing your natural abilities As in everybody's life, people also played a big part in my life, but the kind of people I associated with, for the most part, were people of great character and skill, people who were demonstrably caring, respectful, and visionary. Those are the kind of people I hung around. I didn't hang around with jerks.

I hung around with people who inspired me. I watched what they did and was amazed at what they could do.

For example, I have a friend named Frank who did not attend institutions of higher learning like I did, does not have a college degree like I do, nor a master's degree in finance like me. But when it comes to metal working, machinery, heavy equipment, and welding exotic metals, he can do it all and more. He is the damnedest guy I've ever seen in my life—a shining example of Malcolm Gladwell's thesis that success is all about discovering and developing your natural abilities.

One day, I tore all the skin off my hand trying to charge the battery on my Bobcat. I grounded something. Sparks flew! I bled and called Frank. Frank came over, looked at my hand, and said, "You want me to take you to the hospital?"

I said, "No. I deserve this."

Frank responded, "Well, then, let's fix your Bobcat."

It took him about ten minutes. I asked, "How do you know how to do this?"

He said, "Well, that's the stuff I learned. While you were going to school, I was working, learning my trade. I guess I discovered my natural abilities."

Good Lord a mercy. He can do anything. Amazing guy.

The Greatest Threat to Our Country

One day, I was in Charlotte, North Carolina, giving a presentation to the Charlotte Council on International Affairs. Afterward, I entertained some questions. A young college student majoring in international affairs asked, "Sir, what is the greatest threat to our country?"

I answered him so fast, I surprised myself. I said, "A divided nation. We can handle about anything if we're not divided. But divided, we have serious problems."

When I gave a presentation at Fort Eustis, Virginia, a young person asked me, "Sir, why is it that so many of my generation have become attracted to a socialistic style government?"

I fired back instantly, "Civics." I explained, "Young man, when I was your age, I took a course in civics. Everybody was required to. We talked about the Constitution and the Bill of Rights. We talked about a lot of important subjects that are directly related to our ability to live as free men and women. I travel all over this country, and I'm always asking our teachers and academicians, 'How many hours do your students receive on the principles and practices of liberty?' Most responses are, 'None.' Young man, educate yourself about the perils of socialism. In a nutshell, you don't get to make any decisions when you arrive in that world, and you don't get to complain about it. You do what you're told."

That's exactly why the Founding Fathers fought the war of independence. And here we are, going full circle back to where we started. The people who are in charge, including the rulers of the government, make money, take vacations, and receive the best medical care. Rank-and-file folks like you and me take the hindmost.

I told the young man, "Your reading should include the Jamestown Experiment on communal economics. In that experiment, tillable land was owned by all. Everybody was to plant seed and participate in harvesting the crop in the fall. Of course, the lazy people didn't plant seed. The ones who did plant seed didn't have enough food for everyone. The experiment did not work. So the leaders said, 'We've had enough of communal economics. Here's what we're going to do next year: we're going to carve this land up, and each man's going to own his own plot. You can eat if you plant. If you don't plant, you don't eat. That's called free enterprise.'"

People ask me about the principles and practices of liberty. I tell them, "The greatest threat to our republic is a lack of wisdom and virtue in our elected leaders." Former American Vietnam POW and Congressional Medal of Honor recipient, Vice Admiral James B. Stockdale, put it this way: "Education should take care to illuminate values and not bury them amongst the trivia."

Are our students getting the message that, without personal integrity, intellectual skills are worthless?

Dr. Martin Luther King, Jr., echoed those same sentiments in a 1947 presentation on education, saying the most dangerous criminal may be the man gifted with reason but no morals. Our founders were unanimous in their beliefs that our land would also be a free, self-governing nation if we maintain an adequate national defense and if there is sufficient wisdom and virtue in the people. They did not fear foreign aggression, for they knew the shed blood of American warriors had not and would not let that happen. The greatest threat would come from inadequate wisdom and virtue in the people.

Folks, we are the people. Virtue is a willing sacrifice of one's private interest to serve the greater good of community, of nation. You may recall the words of the late president John F. Kennedy, who said, "Ask not what your country can do for you but what you can do for your country."

Our Founding Fathers understood that with sufficient wisdom and virtue in the people, these values would be exercised in the selection of our leaders so that we do not depend upon their virtue but upon you and me, who choose them. In other words, we the people shall decide which candidates are wise and virtuous. Thomas Jefferson's writing reminds us that virtue is not hereditary. It must be learned, earned, continually cultivated, and passed from one generation to the next. Our founders looked to the homes, schools, and churches to fuel the fires of virtue; but today, those indispensable pillars of support are in serious decay.

Thankfully, one of the last great bastions of virtue resides in the hearts of the men and women who serve our nation in uniform. The armed forces of the United States of America is one of the most prestigious institutions in America, and for good reason. The conduct of our warriors on and off the field of battle is a reminder to every American that the profound ideas and principles upon which the greatest country in human history was built are still there. They work the same way every time they are tried, and they are beckoning all of us to come home and reclaim the promise of America.

So, why are younger generations moving toward socialism? It's because they don't understand what I just shared with you. My wife, Sheila, says that great faith is won on the battlefields of life, and the older we get, the more battlefields we've been in and gone through. We graciously win most of them, but not all of them. With great trials and tribulations come great faith.

Although Americans have had differences of opinion since the founding of our country, it was rare that there was a difference of values. Some felt that we got things done through people and others through the government. One of the founding principles of our country that I value is liberty. If we can't come to agreement that liberty is an important value for America, then we're headed into a hole we can't get out of.

Differences of opinion abound because we're all different, but we can come together as a community, with common values and ethics. We can agree that certain things are taboo in our society, such as prejudice and racism. It is OK to have differences on how to get things done because that's what liberty stands for. If we can get things done through individual effort, we should. If it is better to get something done through the government, we should. We just need to agree on what should be done.

During a particularly difficult time in his corporate history, Jim Petersen, the author of this book, said, "The only way that we will be destroyed is from within." A divided nation can destroy us from within. In other words, we fail when we're divided not by opinions, but by values.

One of the most amazing aspects of the American story was the unanimity of agreement on foundational principles, in spite of coming from widely divergent backgrounds. The common denominator for this near-complete agreement on the big issues was the values they held in common—values that were forged by their life experiences and also by their shared passion to be well-read.

In those days, entertainment was too often ten miles away by mule. A book to read on Saturday night was therefore a big treat. But books were scarce, and the subject matter was invariably focused on history, philosophy, and religious doctrine. Understandably, these books were read over and over, and most importantly, they became the grindstone that sharpened our founders' appetite to live as free men and women. When you get to the point where you can't reach unanimity on the big issues—life, liberty, the pursuit of happiness—you're headed down a rabbit hole that's just going to be hard to crawl out of.

The Prevalence of Post-Traumatic Stress Disorder (PTSD) among Former Prisoners of War in Vietnam

One day, I was at the Air Force academy eating lunch at a table that was subsequently populated by instructors of the leadership and ethics department. They became embroiled in a conversation about PTSD and what was the best way to prevent it and treat it. I suggested to them that they contact the US Navy in Pensacola, Florida, which is the repository on all information for all POWs for all of America's wars. I heard that they completed a study on PTSD, and the ethics and leadership staff might be able to gain some useful information.

Not long after that, I visited Pensacola to have an annual physical because they wanted to update their information on all the Vietnam POWs. I go there once a year, like most of us POWs should do. One of the requirements is that the POWs talk to a psychiatrist. After the psychiatrist quit asking me silly questions about whether I like red or blue, I said, "I have a question for you." I related the experience I had at the academy to the psychiatrist. I said, "You're the expert. How much PTSD did American Vietnam POWs have?" I was curious.

He got up, picked up a folder, and handed me some papers that were clipped together. I read it over. The title was, "A 37-Year Longitudinal Study on Post-Traumatic Stress Disorders for Returning American Vietnam Prisoners of War." The percentage of American POWs diagnosed with PTSD was less than 5 percent. I turned to the psychiatrist and said, "Well, if it's less than five percent, that can be noise. That's almost nothing. The average is thirty percent for returning Vietnam veterans who weren't POWs. So, what's the difference?"

He said, "We call it optimism."

"Is that a medical term?" I asked, trying to kid him.

Incidence of PTSD among US War Veterans

The US Department of Veterans Affairs estimates that PTSD afflicts war veterans as follows:[35]

- Almost 31 percent of Vietnam veterans
- As many as 10 percent of Gulf War (Desert Storm) veterans
- 11 percent of veterans of the war in Afghanistan
- 20 percent of Iraqi war veterans

PTSD is a serious medical condition that is treatable. Getting support is huge. Talk about it. Pray about it.

A young lady recently asked me, "How did you survive your long, dark night of terror in Hanoi?"

I responded, "I was always most at peace in prayer and when I was helping a fellow POW in greater need than myself."

Affiliating with the right group can transform your life. America's warriors quickly learn not to focus on the final score, but only on the play at hand. You cannot be an American warrior of one, a POW of one, a wounded warrior of one, or anything else of one and have much of a chance to endure and prosper. Choosing the correct group can be a game changer for your physical and emotional well-being due to the help you receive from one another.

Conversely, your spiritual well-being, your sense of inner peace and personal contentment, will not be dependent on the help you receive but on the help you are willing to give.

A Trip to the White House, Where I Met John Wayne and the President of the USA

As a returning Vietnam prisoner of war and USAF officer from the East Coast, I was assigned to Andrews Air Force Base to complete an extensive POW physical and debriefing.

---

35 "PTSD: A Growing Epidemic," NIH Medline*Plus*, Winter 2009, https://medlineplus.gov/magazine/issues/winter09/articles/winter09pg10-14.html.

As a courtesy to the returning Vietnam POWs, we were provided escorts to ensure that our large volume of medical and debriefing appointments was accomplished on schedule. I was assigned a very attractive and punctual nurse. No matter how early or late my appointment might be, she made sure I was on time. One morning, she showed up with a dress with these little tie straps in the back and told me to put it on. I asked why. She explained that my procedure required a gown. I explained to her that I was not going to walk down the hospital hallways in a dress with an exposed butt. She finally agreed that I could dress in the room where the procedure would be accomplished.

It wasn't until I arrived at the room that I thought to ask the purpose of my scheduled medical procedure. At that point my attractive companion smiled and said, "It's routine. All of the Vietnam POWs are scheduled for this procedure."

I responded, "That's great. What are we going to do?"

My nurse friend was grinning like a Cheshire cat and said," You are going to have a colonoscopy."

I said, "What the heck is a colonoscopy?" I darn sure didn't know.

She smiled, laughed, regained her composure, and explained the procedure.

My response was clear and forceful: "That is not going to happen. You are delusional. Where are my clothes?"

At that point, my companion nurse began to plead, explaining that the procedure was critical to safeguard my health. Finally, I said, "OK. I will accept this procedure under one condition: you go first."

Three months after my release from North Vietnam's infamous Hỏa Lò prison, I received an invitation from the White House to attend a celebratory dinner for repatriated American Vietnam prisoners of war. I asked my nurse friend to go with me. She accepted. During the cocktail hour, while we were sight-seeing in the White House, I saw President Nixon and my favorite Hollywood warrior, John Wayne, walking side by side, headed directly toward us. I nudged my date and said, "Look who's coming!"

She tensed up and said in an excited whisper, "Is that John Wayne?"

As they approached us, I turned to my date and said, "Watch this!"

I stepped suddenly in front of John Wayne, stopping him in his tracks, and said, "Wayne, where the heck were you when we needed you?"

Breaking into a big smile while looking down on my 5'9" frame from his towering 6'5", and in that classic John Wayne voice, he drawled, "Well, pilgrim, you don't believe that stuff, do you?"

We all broke into laughs and exchanged greetings, and my date received a kiss from President Nixon and the legendary John Wayne. How many ladies can say that?

Someone snapped a photo of us during my visit to the White House.
From the left are my brother, his wife, me, and my niece.

We Touch People's Lives Without Realizing It

Through the years, people have told me they admire me because of what I survived. I don't think I did anything different from what most people would have done. But I learned that my experiences could have a significant impact on others.

After I returned home from Hanoi, I received a letter out of the blue from someone who had attended UNC with me. He wrote, "I have been reminiscing about my years as a University of North Carolina student, and I have been trying to recollect the people I met there who had the most profound and positive impact on my life. Barry, you are at the top of the list. I've never seen such contagious passion, inspiration, and determination. You have had a very positive and profound impact on my life."

About seven years ago, I got another letter from another person who said essentially the same thing. He told me, "You are contagious, passionate, and an inspiration. You have a positive and wonderful influence on my life. Thank you."

We all touch people. We leave our human fingerprints on people's minds and hearts, even though we don't realize it. Remember, a spark can create a fire!

We do not know what the future will bring. We must hold tightly to our values and adapt to whatever life throws at us. We must focus on what we can change and accept the rest with dignity, humor, and patience.

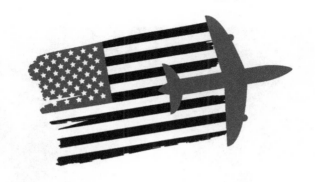

Chapter 13

CHERISH WHAT IS IMPORTANT TO YOU

Jim

Barry has a keen appreciation for all that he was given in life, not the least of which is his family. I often hear him talking about the women who support him, including his wife, Sheila, and their two daughters, Deidra and Courtney. He puts those that he cherishes on a pedestal and speaks about them in glowing terms. This is a lesson we all can benefit from: cherish what is important to you.

Barry

After I left the hospital at Andrews Air Force Base, I entered a major aircraft requalification program for repatriated air force pilots in San Antonio, Texas. Not long after that, I met Ms. Sheila.

The moment I met Sheila, the Chili Queen from Luckenbach, Texas, I knew she was the one for me.

A Bumpy Beginning

During training, Tom, a POW buddy of mine, said to me, "I was recently a judge at the Miss Chilympiad chili-cooking contest. I met a young lady you need to meet." So after work one day, Tom and I went to Southwest Texas State University[36], where Sheila was a student and working in the Physical

---

36 The school was originally called Southwest Texas State Teachers College and changed to Southwest Texas State College. In 1969, it changed again to Southwest Texas State University, which is what it was called when Barry went there. It is now known as Texas State University (www.txstate.edu).

Education (PE) department. It took some begging, but I convinced her to join Tom and me after work at a local bar. We had a great time, and I thought I had impressed her. Boy, was I wrong.

One evening, when I was supposed to have a date with Sheila, I drove over to pick her up, but she wasn't at her apartment. I waited around for a considerable period of time. I was hoping she was OK. Turns out, she had stood me up, so I asked myself, "Is this a message?"

Sheila later explained her intensions were to make the date, but she had a car problem. Early that afternoon she had driven to Lukenbach, Texas, to represent her Chilly Queen title at a fundraiser. She met a guy, danced a few dances and when it was time to drive back, her car would not start. She asked her dance partner if he would give her a lift back to her apartment. He agreed, but on the way back his car radiator overheated. They eventually were able to make it to her apartment but too late for our date. But she never called me. I have a lot of pride. I figured she decided to shove me off to the side. Screw that, so I went back to whatever I was doing. A few days later, my phone rang. Ms. Sheila was on the phone. She said, "Hi."

I responded, "How can I help you?"

She said, "Do you still want to go out dancing?"

I said, "No. I don't want to go dancing."

She pleaded, "Oh, come on. I'll teach you how to dance."

She started cutting up with me a little bit, and I said, "Where the heck were you the other night?"

She told me about her car not starting and the guy's radiator overheating. I told her, "Sheila, I do not appreciate being stood up without somebody telling me what's going on, but I'll go dancing."

That gal was more fun to be with than a barrel of monkeys, and it was always like that. Every time I was with Sheila, I was absolutely elated, happy as a lark.

Sheila smoked cigarettes. After about the third date, I said, "Let me explain something. You don't have to respond to this. You can do anything you wish, but I want you to know that lips that touch cigarettes will never touch mine."

When Sheila graduated, I encouraged her to apply for a job with Delta Airlines as a flight attendant. She did, and after passing a battery of tests and multiple interviews, she was hired and began a six-week training program.

I helped her get ready for her exams. I worked with her on vocabulary, logic sentences—all kinds of different things—for a week or two. She aced everything. I had an ulterior motive: she could fly to see me wherever I was. We did everything together. We hunted, we fished, we field-trialed our Labradors, and we played tennis. We just had a blast—and we still do.

As of August 1, 2020, Sheila retired from Delta Airlines as a flight attendant with forty-six years of service.

The Proposal

In 1979, I was assigned to Ft. Leavenworth to work with the US Army. By now, Ms. Sheila had moved in with me in a little place called Platte City, just outside Kansas City, Missouri. We were living out in the country. Sheila never pushed. One thing I loved about Sheila is that she never demanded anything.

I said to her one day, "You know, we need to get married, but I don't know when it's going to be."

Sheila is from Texas, and she loves the yellow rose of Texas. So I planted some yellow rose bushes in front of our big bay window in the kitchen. My plan was to propose when I saw the first yellow rose bloom. I didn't know when it was going to happen; It was in God's hands.

One morning, I walked into the kitchen and saw that one yellow rose had bloomed. I told Sheila, "Come with me."

I took her outside and sat her on the stoop, right in front of the yellow rose bloom. Then I called TriStar, our Labrador, who was sitting out of sight holding the engagement ring box. He came on a dead run and sat down in front of Sheila. Sheila took the box from his mouth and opened it.

Boom. That's how we got engaged in the spring of 1979 and followed by our wedding in November of that year.

It was a huge wedding held in Sheila's hometown in Ennis Texas, south of Dallas. We had ten bridesmaids and groomsmen, and we invited about four hundred people. It was a Czech wedding because that's Sheila's heritage. The wedding was at 2:00 in the afternoon, and we were still dancing at midnight.

Everybody wanted to dance with Sheila. I don't know how she did it. Good Lord have mercy. Unbelievable, she might as well have run an Olympic Marathon.

One of the happiest days of my life—the day Sheila married me.

Our Daughters, Deidra and Courtney

Sheila and I are blessed to have two daughters, Deidra and Courtney. We taught both girls to hunt and fish at an early age. They love the outdoors and are great athletes.

A good way to understand our girls is to check out what they value about life, about living, about being. You will discover their values reflect the upbringing and values of both Sheila and me.

Deidra, our first daughter, was born at Fort Leavenworth, Kansas, on August 7, 1983. Her arrival was quite exciting. In the middle of the night, Sheila's water broke. Sheila's version is that she woke me up, and I started bouncing off the walls. Sheila said, "What are you doing?"

According to Sheila, I said, "I don't know. What am I supposed to do?"

Sheila replied, "Take me to the hospital."

Now, here's *my* version of what happened. When Sheila's water broke, she said, "Oh, Barry! My water just broke!"

I was in a deep sleep. I was trying to wake up, and she said, "We've got to go to the hospital!"

I took that to mean we had to get to the hospital as fast as possible. I rushed to the closet and couldn't find our pre-packed hospital bag.

Sheila asked, "What are you *doing*?"

I said, "What do I do? What do I do? What do I do?"

I said it three times—and fast—because I was moving fast.

We got into the car, and while I was hauling butt to the hospital, I looked in the rearview mirror, and sure enough, there came Smokey Bear with his red and blue lights flashing. I pulled over and jumped out of the car. The policeman had jumped out of his patrol car, too and was shouting, "Stop, stop, stop!"

I said, "My wife's having a baby! Her water broke!"

The policeman walked over to the car, looked at Sheila, and said, "Follow me."

Sheila was strong, so I advised the doctors not to give her any medication for pain. Sheila was screaming the F-word at me. I was telling her, "You can do this." I was squeezing her hand and saying, "All right. Push. Push!"

Sheila screamed, "Get your butt out of here!"

She'd had enough of that. Deidra popped out, and she was a blue baby. I didn't care what color she was, as long as she was healthy. We called her "Snookie Buns."

Courtney, our second child, was born on March 17, 1988. Two weeks before Sheila's due date, she met with our CPA to finalize our taxes. At the very moment he revealed the total taxes we owed—*kaboom!*—Sheila's water broke. Not only that—it was St. Patrick's Day, and a slow-moving parade interfered with our ability to speed to the hospital. The streets were crowded with people and floats. Once again, the police came to the rescue. I saw a cop and told him, "Hey, my wife's water broke, and she's having a baby!"

He said, "Follow me." He escorted us right through the parade to the hospital. Another exciting birth!

Sheila did the bulk of the child rearing, but we were both engaged with those girls up to our ears. Both excelled academically and athletically. At one time, our older daughter, Deidra, was on three basketball teams. She also excelled in volleyball and track. Courtney was also quite the athlete in her own right in volleyball, basketball, track, and cross-country.

Courtney was valedictorian of her class. Both daughters were awarded the scholar-athletic medal in their senior year. Both girls grew up into responsible wives and mothers and have blessed us with awesome grandchildren. There is great joy in being able to influence your children to appreciate that what you *earn* will make you a living, but what you *give* will make you a life. We look forward to leaving a legacy that will help our children and theirs to become responsible human beings and, hopefully, to weather any storm they might face.

Sheila Takes the Lead in Parenting

When I transitioned into the financial services industry, I was working long hours. I'd get home around 8:00 or 9:00 p.m. many nights. I worked during all holidays except for Christmas and Mother's Day. As a result, Sheila was doing most of the work with the girls.

One night, I pulled up to the house around 9:00 p.m. As I started to get out of the truck, the side door to the house opened. Sheila came flying out to the driveway with her hand in the air, running toward the truck. As I stepped out of my truck, I raised my hand.

She screamed, "You're in, damn it!"

It was my turn, now, to take care of the girls. Evidently, they weren't doing what they should have been doing. When I walked into the house, Courtney was sitting there with her math book. I said, "OK, Courtney, what are you working on?"

She said, "Exponents."

I said, "Give me a pencil and a piece of paper." I hadn't taken my bag off my shoulder yet.

For the next twenty minutes, I drilled her on the laws of exponents and gave her problems to solve.

Then I said, "You're good. Deidra, come over here. Bring a pencil and paper. What are you working on?"

That's how we interacted with our daughters. Sheila was blessed at the time because Delta Airlines had an auxiliary program for flight attendants, and she flew only two trips a month—and that was considered full time. She was gone only six days a month, which helped immensely. We didn't have daycare, so when Sheila was flying, we had to find people to watch the girls.

For four years, while Deidra played sports, Sheila was the "mother" of the basketball and volleyball teams. She had to coordinate all the meals and organize the teams, as parents tend to do. When Deidra finished, Courtney followed, causing Sheila to repeat her role as mother of the teams. They both played on the varsity teams as freshmen in high school.

Courtney was extraordinarily responsible. During home football games at Platte City, a designated teacher was required to be on duty for the game to handle administrative duties. One day, Courtney was designated as the "teacher" who would be on duty for the game, even though she was still a student in high school. The superintendent was fine with that. That was the attitude the teachers had about Courtney. During her senior year of high school, she was the class president, as well as the student-body president, and was voted Prom Queen.

Courtney exhibited some of the same characteristics as my mom. She encouraged others to get things done by showing them how to do it. She didn't chastise them or yell at them when there was a large project to get done in high school. She was thoughtful and caring.

One day, Courtney told Sheila, "Mom, I'm going to pole-vault." Courtney is about 5'4". She was not nearly as tall as most pole-vaulters.

Sheila said, "No way. You're going to kill yourself."

But I encouraged Courtney to do it.

Sheila repeated, "She's gonna kill herself."

Courtney ended up becoming a pole-vaulter, and she tied the high-school record for girls. She did not kill herself.

Courtney made us proud by getting accepted to the University of North Carolina. At the time, they accepted only 18 percent of out-of-state applicants. Also, she was accepted into the Kenan-Flagler Business School. She excelled in school and spent a year in Tai Pei, Taiwan, so she could learn Mandarin Chinese.

Our family vacationed in Hawaii in July 2005. From left are Courtney, Sheila, me, and Deidra.

Deidra (Bridger) Johnson's Thoughts about Her Dad

Jim

Here, Barry and Sheila's older daughter, Deidra, shares her perspective about having Barry as her dad.

Deidra

My dad was strict. I would classify his parenting style as one of high expectations, structure, obedience, and respect that often came in the form of a lecture. The lectures were usually brief, philosophical, and profound.

When I was in trouble, my dad would use terms like "penalize" and "under restriction"—it was his military background coming out. It always made me laugh. He'd say, "You are penalized." I would ask him what that meant. None of my friends' parents talked like that. Dad was the enforcer.

Passionate, Dedicated Parents

Academics and athletics were at the forefront of my parents' efforts in raising us. Both my sister and I were scholar athletes of our graduating classes. Our parents were dedicated to laying a good foundation for us by encouraging us to get involved with sports.

We started mixed martial arts and T-ball at a young age. Some of my most vibrant childhood memories recall our backyard competition of who could hit the ball off the stand over the biggest, tallest tree in the backyard. And they cleared the basement to roll out a big Judo mat. Vivid is my recollection of practices and reading books about Judo technique. They coached our softball traveling team and even hosted the team of girls in our family travel trailer for some tournaments. This morphed into Amateur Athletic Union (AAU) travel to basketball games and camps all over the country.

When high school began, it was volleyball, cross-country, basketball, and track. Mom and Dad hardly missed a game and sometimes even came to the practices. They were incredibly passionate about giving us great athletic experiences, knowing the virtue it would bestow on us in our adult lives.

The great outdoors was a big focal point of their parenting style. They're both adventurous and have an outdoorsy spirit. They complemented each other because they both love camping, hunting, fishing, and the great outdoors. Daddy was a prolific bird caller, and without any manufactured calls—just his own mouth! Ducks, turkey, quail, owl. Perhaps I first realized the majesty of the woods off the back patio, Daddy projecting his barred owl calls into the sixteen acres of lush Midwest forest. I can still hear their fierce, melodious vocal dueling today. I cherish all the memories of turkey hunting and crappie fishing off his jet boat and that he encouraged his daughters to get in the woods and on the water.

Indeed, a strong foundation and passion for the great outdoors was instilled early on that grew to land me both a career and husband! We run a fishing charter business in southwest Florida. For five years, I was the First Mate and helped run the boat, rig rods, catch bait, bait hooks, and entertain clients. We have been very involved with TV shows, radio interviews, magazine articles, -pro-staff duties, philanthropic events, and the tournament world. Now that we have a child, I'm in charge of marketing, bookings, financials, social media, the website, and video editing for YouTube. I credit my folks for laying a foundation for my career success.

Learning about Daddy's POW Experience

I was likely in the eighth grade or a freshman in high school when I learned that my dad had been a prisoner of war in Vietnam. Daddy used to pace back and forth in the basement in the pitch-black dark, talking to himself. I thought he was completely nuts. I had no idea he was practicing speeches to present to large groups of people.

It wasn't until college, when I chose to deliver his POW speech for Speech class, that I truly fully appreciated what my dad went through. This experience really drove it all in. After that, he allowed me to work alongside him to update his PowerPoint slides and jazz up his presentations. That increased my respect and admiration for my dad.

I was inspired to read some books written by his fellow POWs. When I was in college, my sister and I read one of them together—Ed Hubbard's book called *Escape from the Box*. It changed Courtney's life. Both of us continued to read POW books that were in my dad's library. These books provided great insight, fascination, and sorrow for what my father successfully endured. It caused him to positively uplift and impact countless lives, and that has been a tremendous blessing to experience. That's probably my greatest takeaway from coming to understand what my dad went through.

My dad has always been very humble. He never projected himself to be a victim throughout the POW experience. He has never been very emotional about what he went through. He is more matter-of-fact about it, saying, "This is what we did, and this is how we endured. My faith got me through it." He is a big-picture person who doesn't get into the nitty-gritty of his emotions and feelings. As a matter of fact, I've never seen my father cry. He is very strong, very stoic.

Faith, Vocabulary, and Thinking

The Christian religion is a big part of our family. My mom was the driver here. We were part of a new nondenominational church that started out in a middle-school gym and is massive today. We went every Sunday, but Daddy would sometimes opt out of going to church because he would take Jesus fishing.

Often, we would find our dad on his knees, praying. He has a very deep connection with Jesus, and that's what got him through his POW experience.

Some of the life lessons I learned from my dad were the value of vocabulary and communication skills. We had the "vocabulary word of the day," and he would play a game when he was driving us to school. He would say, "Hi, Deidra, I'm Billy. I don't understand what this word means. Can you use a synonym?" We called it the "Billy vocabulary game."

Fast-forward, and as a young adult establishing my career, I made it a point to listen to vocabulary CDs in the car. One of the biggest gifts I gave my dad was a vocabulary journal that I wrote. I felt that the greatest gift I could ever give my parents was showing them that I applied myself and that I used the skills and the foundation they demonstrated to me.

One of my father's' most admirable traits is his ability to use his mind, no doubt attributed to his time in Vietnam. One day, I walked into our computer nook, and my dad was sitting in the chair, staring up at the ceiling. I was a teenager, and I said, "Why are you just sitting there and staring?"

He looked at me and said, "Young lady, I'm thinking. You need to take time to think."

I thought, "I do think. What are you talking about?"

Now I feel like thinking is a lost skill in today's fast-paced, time-poor society. How many times do people just stop and try to think through things? People are constantly on the go, complaining about this and that, and Googling everything to see what other people think. People don't just step back and use their God-given skills sometimes.

I know that in Vietnam, Daddy had a lot of time to think. He was able to solve so many problems just by using what was upstairs. in his head.

I was a successful basketball player who played through college. When I was in high school, my dad calculated the optimal degree, alignment, and velocity for a three-point shot. To ensure that I threw the perfect shot, he had a ring welded on a stand that I had to shoot through. It worked because I won the Nebraska three-point shootout. I don't think there's another dad in the country who would do that. It just shows you what you can do with your mind.

Another example of my dad using his mind is when he learned architecture software to do a massive home remodel. He knew he could calculate the angles using trigonometry and calculus—a skill he used often as a POW. One day while in captivity, John McCain tapped over and asked, "Can you calculate the degree at which the sun sets on any given day?"

Although Daddy didn't have trig tables, he persisted at solving the equation.

A year later, he tapped back, "John, I got it!" And thirty years later, he conquered the home remodel and designed the Solstice room. It consists of three panels facing west. When the sun sets, the light is directly in the middle of each panel, according to the solstices and the equinoxes. I think that is such a rewarding way of using your God-given abilities, fine-tuned in the midst of immeasurable tribulation.

My Dad's Integrity and Determination

I tear up sometimes when I think about my dad's integrity. He is all about taking action. Immediate, unwavering, confident, decisive action is something my dad does so well. He has a saying: "Move, or you're all going to die" and "You'd never make a good fighter pilot." He stressed to us that you can't be indecisive. You can't sit around when it's time to make an important decision.

One day, my daddy and I were returning from my sister's soccer game and were in the middle of a conversation. On a two-lane road, a car passed another car when approaching a hill. Unfortunately, we were coming the other way on the other side of the hill. To prevent a head-on collision and to prevent the car from flipping down a steep embankment, my dad whipped the car onto the shoulder, perfectly balancing between the oncoming car and the embankment. He then whipped the car back into his lane. It was eerie. It was unbelievable. His ability to do this comes from flying fighter jets—and probably his faith in the Lord. His faith in Jesus came through, and an angel took over.

Another intense experience for me was in the fourth grade. I cut my hand badly on a roller gate. My mom rushed me to the hospital; my hand was just hanging there. It was traumatizing for me. My mom called my dad. He rushed to the hospital to help me. The doctor said he was going to have to amputate three of my fingers. My dad said, without hesitation, "No. Put her in that ambulance and take her to KU (Kansas University) Medical Center right now."

They did not respond quickly enough, so Daddy got in their faces and said, "Do it—*now!*"

Everybody stopped in their tracks and said, "OK." They did it immediately. My dad didn't know it at the time, but the best hand specialist in the country was at the KU Medical Center. To this day, Daddy doesn't know why he said that. He has these divine-intervention abilities. Dad is decisive, and he saves lives as a result. It's one of his great character traits.

One time when we were flying to North Carolina for Christmas, a snowstorm came through and shut down the airport. Daddy said, "We're driving." We walked out of the airport, got into the car, and started driving to North Carolina from Missouri. When we got to Kentucky, we got swallowed up by a snowstorm. The whole interstate was shut down, helicopters were everywhere assisting accident victims, and everything was at a standstill. Cars were running out of gas.

Daddy said, "Screw this, I'm not sitting here." He off-roaded through the woods. He was the only person to do it. Everyone else was just sitting there. No, not Daddy. He found a way to get off that interstate and get us all to safety.

My favorite childhood story was about my kitty cat that I rescued and named Meow when I was very young. She climbed up a tree in one of the famous Midwest tornado thunderstorms. I wanted her rescued immediately. Daddy climbed up the tree in the storm and rescued Meow.

As he grabbed Meow, she stuck her claw in Daddy's eye. Daddy did not projectile-launch the cat, which is probably what I would have done. He salvaged his little girl's baby kitty cat and also saved his eye. If the claw had hit his eye differently, he would have lost his sight. He handled it well, probably because of trauma he endured leading up to these types of moments.

Dad encouraged us to do our best and complete the task at hand. He would say, "Don't ever think you can get out of your work and not finish what you started. Always do your best."

One day when I was in the fifth grade, he was babysitting me while Mom was on a trip. He came into my bedroom and said, "Did you do all your homework?"

I told him, "It's good enough."

He said, "Absolutely not." He brought me out of my room, even though it was 9:30 p.m., past my bedtime. He sat there as I completed my homework.

And to this day, I am motivated to "carry my burdens till dark," as Daddy likes to say.

From left to right: Deidra, Gage, and Bo Johnson

Daddy's wall of WISDOM

 Focus on developing your **Mind, Body,** and **Spirit**... and the rest will take care of itself

4 things

As ye believe....

Walk in the Spirit
Do your part
Keep your eye on the ball
Practice brevity in all you do

Too soon old, too late smart

If you don't quit, what do you have to regret?
.... and if you do quit, what do you have to celebrate?

What you earn will make you a living.......what you give will make you a life

ATTENTION TO DETAIL

You do not measure one's success in what you earn for yourself,
but rather how much you help others to achieve for themselves

Fear not the things of man - - Fear the things of God .... FRET NOT!!

What u have inherited from
your forefathers, earn over for yourself,
or it will not be yours

Good JUDGEMENT

Short-term satisfaction.... Long-term disaster

Gotta have a PLAN!...but then "plan" on that PLAN changing!

**WISH THINGS WERE THE WAY THEY ARE....
AND STILL CARRY ON WELL**

The Lord gave you this [   ], don't use this ____

Deidra put together this poster board; she calls it "Daddy's Wall of Wisdom."
It contains many of the nuggets of wisdom Barry has imparted to her throughout her life.

Courtney (Bridger) Isernhagen's Thoughts about Her Dad

Jim

Barry and Sheila's younger daughter, Courtney, shares her perspective about having Barry as her dad.

Courtney

Since I can remember, my father has been a man of routine. I still recall our evening ritual, prior to my entering grade school. I'd anxiously wait for him to pull up the drive and immediately fall in line behind him as he marched into the house and down the hall. He'd put me up on the highest part of the closet shelf so we could discuss our day as he hung up his coat and tie. The best part of the night was when he'd pull me off the shelf and throw me on the king-sized waterbed repeatedly until Mom yelled at us to come eat dinner.

Engaged, Involved Parents

Both of my parents were very engaged in my life. Both had very specific and distinct roles. Mother ensured we were up on time, decently dressed per the weather, and maintained good behaviors and manners. Father assumed the role of ensuring we were studious pupils and consistently bringing a relentless positive attitude and effort to every sports practice. Father's second-most-played role was stepping in the second we were not obeying Mother—something Deidra and I tried our best to avoid at every cost. His ability to stand up and take a single step still intimidates me to this day.

With Mother being a flight attendant (working typically three days out of town at a time) and Father being a financial planner (having client meetings outside office hours), you'd think they'd miss the majority of our extracurricular activities. Surprisingly, Mother did a phenomenal job of coordinating schedules to where I rarely recall a single practice, let alone game, where one of them was not present. One high school track practice still comes to mind this day where my father just happened to be present the day of repeat 400s (full laps around the track). Approximately seven laps in, my father had the audacity to yell at me in front of the entire team, fifty kids or so, and ask me why I was loafing.

Growing up with my father, loafing was not an option. You might think he was this way just toward sports, but lucky for Deidra and me, it was with every facet of our existence.

One night, I was completing a research for a sixth-grade history project. The electricity went out, thus Netscape (the original Google), so I decided to pack up for the evening. This was unacceptable for my father, for we just happened to own a set of Britannica encyclopedias. Out came the flashlight, and the research continued. Fortunately for me, the batteries in the flashlight quickly died. With no extra D-cells laying around, I again proceeded to pack up. Wrong again. My father gladly whipped out the kerosene lantern and accompanied me at the kitchen table until my research was complete.

Unfortunately for my fourteen-year-old son, I possess much of my father's never-give-up attitude. I have been known to accompany him while he cranks out his own homework in front of the campfire while we're enjoying a weekend getaway.

Learning about My Dad's Wartime Experiences

I was in the second grade when my father conducted a surprise presentation to my entire class. Eighty of us ten-year-olds were sitting in the hallway when, from behind us, my father came walking up in his full flight suit and helmet. It was in this uniform that my father presented to my classmates several pictures and stories from his prisoner of war experience. While I cannot recall any specific statements he made, I still have classmates approach me to this day asking if I remember my dad walking out in his flight suit.

When I entered my twenties and thirties, my father's six and a half years of experiences became more gut-wrenching as I could better correlate his life with my own. At the age when I was starting a career, starting a family, my father was in a prison cell. At the same age as I was having anniversary dinners with my husband and celebrating birthdays with my children, my father was in a prison cell.

While my father cuts loose and tells incredibly entertaining Vietnam stories in front of a group, rest assured, he's not as open with the immediate family. In my words, not his, I believe there is a plethora of Vietnam stories that have never been told and never will be told. These are the stories my father refuses to tell, but rightfully so, as there is no positive message behind them. For my father, if the story does not have an impactful message behind it that can impart wisdom, then it is not worth telling.

Learning Life Lessons

As I mentioned before, my father was and is a man of routine. When I was young, without even knowing it, my father was teaching me this life lesson as well. He taught me life lessons at such a young age that they stuck with me over the years.

For example, every summer from the time I was about eight years old through the age of fifteen or so, my father presented me a unique basketball challenge. One year, it was ten thousand layups. Another year, it was ten thousand free throws. Fortunately—or unfortunately, depending on how you look at it—I also inherited my father's stubborn side and wasn't about to let a challenge go unclaimed. I now know that my father was teaching me that you must repeat an action ten thousand times to really master the skill.

Integrity and a Perennially Positive Mind-Set

As far as integrity is concerned, my dad always quoted others regarding this subject. He didn't talk about his own integrity. He wouldn't say, "Oh, because I was in the Vietnam War and I survived, I can tell you how or show you how to persevere." He would quote the great philosophers, such as Epictetus and Socrates. He often stated Epictetus's quote, **"Wish things were the way they are, and still carry on well."**

I would repeat these sayings, and they gave me a positive mind-set.

My father's life is a product of his work, his independence, and the experiences he had once the Bridger family adopted him. I want folks to know that's just inherently the individual that he is. He doesn't turn that on and off. He just has this ability to always think positively. His ability to stay positive is something that he enjoys showing to others.

My Mom Is My Dad's Strong Supporter

My mom has been a phenomenal rock for my dad. She always provided what we needed and cared for dad. That has allowed my dad to continue to be who he is. The reason why my dad was able to get away for a full day to hunt or fish and fulfill his spirit to function is that my mom would take on everything else.

My mom is very structured, organized, and detail-oriented. I inherited these traits from her. She does a phenomenal job at keeping things organized.

I think my mom really enjoys the empty-nest syndrome. Finally, she can focus more on that what she likes to do. She has a beautiful yard and great flowers. She didn't do any of that when we were growing up because she didn't have time. My mom's demeanor and her ability to prioritize and focus on the right things have enhanced her relationship with my dad. They are incredibly supportive of each other.

Likewise, when my mom wanted to fly as a flight attendant to Rio de Janeiro for three days and sit on the beach, my dad did all the things he needed to do. My parents have a wonderful dynamic in terms of being able to tag-team. That's so important in taking care of a household and raising children.

When I was younger, I used to love putting on my mom's old flight-attendant uniforms and prancing around the house. I would get sad because I was unable to go with my mom on "take your daughter to work" day.

One year, my mom said, "Screw it. You're going to go to work with me." She specifically booked a trip over "take your kid to work" day. She let me serve the first-class passengers. That was before 9/11. I guarantee you, that wouldn't fly now. I must've been six years old, and I was serving these wonderful passengers in first-class their fancy meal with fancy silverware.

My mom was great at entertaining my sister and me with exciting things to do.

My dad grew up in a family who was well to do and was able to afford much. My mother grew up in a family of five brothers and limited financial resources. Even to this day, my mom penny-pinches, which is how she was raised. I respect that because she does not want to lavishly spend money, even though she could. My sister and I joke because she could use a wardrobe update. She still wears T-shirts from the '90s. She likes them. My mom is very true to her roots: just working hard for every dollar and then holding onto those dollars.

As I live my life and raise children of my own, I think back to things my dad and mom taught me when I was ten years old. I sincerely appreciate my parents imparting much wisdom so that as I live my own life, I can continue to improve the person I am and improve the life I live as a wife and mother.

From left to right: Jamen, Joel, Emma, Ava, and Courtney Isernhagen in September 2020.

Chapter 14

DISCOVER UNCONDITIONAL LOVE

Jim

The following statement is attributed to Will Rogers: "If there are no dogs in heaven, then when I die, I want to go where they went."

I suspect that Barry would say the same, given his strong affiliation with the dogs that were constantly a part of his life. Barry's early adoption days included a new puppy, Duke. He never forgot the unconditional love he felt from Duke and all the dogs he has had over the years—including twelve Black Labrador Retrievers.

Dog owners know that a dog is a calming influence. Barry needed this kind of influence throughout his life, so he surrounded himself with dogs. Barry shared a special bond with his canine companions throughout his life. Here are some of his memories of his beloved pets.

This is another priceless lesson for all of us: discover unconditional love, and embrace it.

Barry

I had only one friend in the orphanage, Billy; and when I lost him, I never forgot how much that hurt. When I was first exposed to a puppy, Duke, by my adoptive family, he became my friend, and I was never going to be without one. Dogs—all animals—will teach you so much about life.

Duke and I were inseparable. The moment I met him, we became best friends. I have always had a dog ever since then.

Duke the Quail-Pointing English Shepherd

I've always had Black Labs, except for Duke, the first dog I had. Duke was an English Shepherd. He was a dog my parents bought for me; but after Duke I always chose Black Labs.

I absolutely adored my dogs because they were my friends. After my experiences in the orphanage and the loss of Billy, I said I'm never going to be without a friend again? I could really relate to my dogs. In fact, a lot of what I experienced in the orphanage is something that a dog can appreciate. When I was about six or seven, I was walking along a country road with my dog, Duke, carrying an air rifle. I noticed a kid standing along the edge of the road close to his house. He had a stick. As I walked up with my dog, Duke, the kid said, "I'm going to throw this stick at your dog."

I replied, "You throw that stick at my dog, and you're not going to like the results."

He threw the stick and hit Duke just below the eye. Blood started spewing out. Duke took off for the house. The kid ran for the front door of his home; but didn't have time to open it. We ran around and around his house three times and I got off three shots, all in his back. On the fourth circle as we were passing the front of his house, the door opened.

His daddy stepped out and grabbed me, lifted me up to break my neck, and said, "I ain't even going to talk to you" and dropped me. I started back home, and I was still fricking mad about what that kid had done to Duke. His dad got into his car and as he drove past me, I shot his windshield.

By the time I got to the house, I had made quite a name for myself. I figured I was going to be in the brig for about six months. But I did what I did out of my attachment for Duke. His dad and my dad confronted me at my house. I said, "Your boy threw a stick that hit my dog. You want to see my dog?" I took them to see Duke.

The kid's dad said, "I'll talk to my boy."

My dad said to me, "That doesn't excuse your shooting the kid in the back with a gosh damn air rifle."

I said, "Well, I didn't use a shotgun."

I wasn't stupid. I knew not to shoot the kid in the head. I knew what to do, and putting knots on his head was not OK. So, I popped him about three times in the back.

That event occurred in early spring. When summer came, I was standing in front of that kid's house again with my air rifle and Duke. This kid wasn't about to throw a stick at Duke anymore. He decided it wasn't worth it. He looked at me, and said, "Does your dog kill rats?"

I said, "He'll do anything."

The kid said, "We've got a lot of rats."

"Show me." We walked behind his house, and there was a ditch bank that was about forty yards long. The entire bank was covered with big rat holes. I looked at the holes and said, "Duke."

Duke went to the first hole and started digging. The rat came out, and Duke snapped its neck. He ended up killing nine rats, one after the other. The kid was amazed. We continued cleaning out the rat holes. I got to shoot some while Duke was killing the rest. Duke dug up that whole bank and cleaned the whole area of rats. This family became the best of friends with Duke and me. Dogs were some of my best friends. Duke was my first amazing pup. He even pointed quail. When I was just eight years old, I got a legal limit of quail all by myself, with my .410 shotgun. However if you throw a stick at my dog, you're going to fight with me, too.

Dog Whisperer

According to one of my nieces, I am among the most incredible dog whisperers in the world. If I could think of it my dogs could do it. For example, I would throw a golf ball into the swimming pool, which was eleven feet deep. My beloved Labs would swim all the way down to the bottom like an otter, pick up the ball, swim back to the surface, give the ball to me, and wait for the next throw. Prior to my deployment to fly combat missions over North Vietnam, I became fast friends with a Veterinarian in Tampa Florida. My vet friend was smart as a whip, and, like me, loved the great outdoors. He fell in love with my Lab Lobo. Here are some reasons why.

One day, Fred and I went duck hunting with Lobo. Fred and I stood up and shot as some ducks came in. His duck fell to our left, and my duck fell to the right, about seventy-five yards apart. Lobo took off running, hit the water, and started after one of the ducks. Fred asked, "How are we going to get that other duck?"

I said, "That isn't going to be a problem."

Fred asked, "Will Lobo respond to hand signals?"

I said, "We don't need to do that. Just watch."

Lobo headed for the first duck and grabbed it in his mouth. Then he immediately made a hard turn in the direction of the second bird. When he got to that one, he changed his grip on the first duck, grabbed the second one in his mouth, and swam back with both ducks. I smiled and said, "Lobo came up with that idea himself."

My dogs could do anything.

The only time I didn't have a dog with me was when I was at Carolina going to school. But in high school and after college, I always had a dog by my side and was constantly training them. I've had eleven Labrador Retrievers—all black. That shows you how dedicated I am to Labs. Not long ago, we lost a lab named Tracker. I said to my wife, "How in the world are we going to replace Tracker?"

Sheila said, "How many Labradors have you had?"

"Eleven," I said.

"She said, "How many of them were duds?"

"None."

"What does that tell you?"

I replied, "I need a puppy. It's the relationship that counts."

She said, "Just like a kid. Dogs are no different."

Now we have a Lab named Spartan. We call him Spartacus.

The Incredible Story of Lobo One

One of the most remarkable things about one of my beloved Labs happened when I was shot down while flying combat over North Vietnam.

Fred offered to keep Lobo for me while I was flying combat missions in Vietnam. I anticipated my combat tour would last about a year - Surprise, I was shot down, captured by the North Vietnamese, and held as a POW for six and a half years.

I later found out that after Fred had kept Lobo for about two years, one of my pilot buddies, who left the service early, said to Fred, "Why don't you let me take Lobo? He deserves to be somewhere besides in a cage. Barry would want us to do this."

So, when he left the US Air Force, my pilot buddy took Lobo out to his expansive property in Midland, Texas. Lobo had the run of an incredible forest and yard. He lived there for three years and passed away of natural causes. By the time I returned, Lobo had been deceased for about a year.

When I finally returned to the US of A after being gone for a total of eight years, I was taken to Andrews Air Force Base Hospital in Maryland. They put me and other POWs who had been released through about thirty hours of intelligence debriefing and gave us extensive physical exams. Finally, I arrived back home in Bladenboro. Soon after that, I decided to go down to Florida to visit my veterinarian friend, Fred and his family.

When I arrived at Fred and his wife, Marilyn's home, a lot of mutual friends were all gathered in their living room. Everyone was asking me lots of questions about what happened in North Vietnam. Then, suddenly, Fred became very quiet, and said, "Barry, I have a story to tell you that you need to hear and you're not going to believe."

I said, "Oh, OK. What's that?"

Fred said, "Well, one night, I got a phone call from my night watchman, who took care of my vet clinic. He was frantic. He almost screamed to me, 'Doc, you've got to get down here quick!' I said to him, 'Charlie, what's wrong?' And he said, 'Come down quick. Lobo is going crazy.' So I got in the car and drove very quickly to the clinic. Charlie met me at the door. He said, 'Hurry! Lobo has lost his mind.' We literally ran through the clinic to the dog kennels. When I arrived at the pen that Lobo was in, he was sitting very quietly with his head held high in the air, staring straight ahead. He paid Charlie and me absolutely no mind. He was in a zone, locked and stiff, unresponsive."

Fred continued the story. He said, "I thought Lobo had suffered a stroke, so I opened up the cage door and began to analyze his situation. I took him into the surgery room and continued my assessment. I could not find anything wrong with Lobo. So we put him back in his kennel. The next morning, I got a phone call from your family telling me you had been shot down over North Vietnam. Other air crews reported your aircraft had sustained a direct hit by a surface-to-air missile. No parachutes were seen, no beepers were heard. Your family was informed that your status was listed as missing in action, probably killed in action, and not to expect that you survived such a horrific explosion. I took the time to convert your shoot-down time over North Vietnam to Eastern Standard Time and discovered, incredibly, that Lobo went berserk at precisely the moment of your shoot-down. The moment your life was in great peril, Lobo began to bang his head against the side of his cage, howl uncontrollably, and lapse into a catatonic state."

Dogs are incredible sentient beings. They provide unconditional love and priceless companionship.

Lobo Dos (Lobo Two), a Reincarnated Physicist

When I returned from the war, the people in my hometown of Bladenboro presented me with a Black Lab puppy. I named him Lobo Dos, or Lobo 2, because he followed my wonderful first Lobo.

In my mind, Lobo Dos was a reincarnated physicist. He was so smart. I taught him to pick up any trash that he found in the house and put it in the trash can so I wouldn't have to pick it up. One day, I couldn't find my wallet. I asked

Sheila, "Did you see my wallet? Where'd I put it?" We began looking all over the house for my wallet and couldn't find it. I stood there wondering how in the heck did I lose my wallet.

Then, suddenly, Sheila said, "Lobo!" She walked over to the nearest trash can, and there was my wallet in the trash.

I gave Lobo a little lecture. I said, "Lobo, we need to talk. You must learn how to distinguish between a wallet and trash. Let's sit down and talk this through."

He had the funniest look in his eyes, as if to say, "You've got to be kidding me."

Be careful what you teach your dogs to do.

Here I am with Lobo Dos, or Lobo 2, the reincarnated physicist. The wonderfully supportive people in my hometown of Bladenboro, North Carolina, gave Lobo 2 to me as a gift when I came home from Vietnam.

Lobo's Theatrical Debut

After my repatriation and requalification in jet aircraft, I was assigned to the 43rd Tactile Fighter Squadron at Goldsboro, North Carolina. One day, I received a phone call from a lady who was producing a high-school theatrical play titled *King Arthur*. She said, "I have been told that you have a Labrador retriever that is very smart. We're looking for a dog to be in our *King Arthur* play. Do you think we might be able to use him?"

I asked, "Where are you located?"

She told me the location." I said, "Why don't I come over there and see what you're doing, and then we'll decide whether or not Lobo can do it?"

She said, "That will be wonderful."

So I went over for the afternoon rehearsal. Some actors were wearing armor, and all were practicing their lines. The producer who called me met me at the back of the theatre. I said, "So, what would you like him to do?"

She responded, "On command, we want him to run down the theatre isle to the stage. He must climb stairs to get onto the stage, walk over to the knight who called him, and sit down. The command will be, 'Lobo, come forth.'"

I thought about that for a second and said, "What about this? The knight says, 'Lobo, come forth.' Lobo will run down the aisle at top-rate speed. You won't need stairs. He'll jump almost five feet in the air and land on the stage. He'll run over to the knight, and if the knight holds out his left arm, Lobo will jump into in his arms."

She said, "Will he do that?" I motioned to the knight on the stage to hold out his left arm and call, "Lobo come forth."

When he called, I said "Lobo, go."

Lobo ran down the aisle, leaped onto the stage, jumped into the air, and landed in the knight's arms. The knight dropped him. Lobo was bewildered, got off the ground, and looked around as if he were asking, "Are you putting me on?"

I then said, "Let's do that again."

I talked to the knight and showed him how to catch a dog. The second time, Lobo and the knight executed the jump and catch perfectly. Unfortunately, the next day, my squadron commander told me that I had to go on a mission to Arizona with three other F-4 Phantoms. So I would not be available to attend any of the performances. The play director said, "What are we going to do if you're not here?"

I said, "After the knight says, 'Lobo, come forth,' you say, 'Lobo, go!' That's all you need to do."

"Will he do that?" she asked.

I replied, "Absolutely."

I left on my mission and returned a week later. The article in the newspaper said it all: "The play *King Arthur* was a big hit, and the Labrador retriever Lobo stole the show." The cast and play director were elated.

Jim

Barry's wife, Sheila, said she fell in love with Lobo before she fell in love with Barry. Lobo would jump over Barry's back or through his arms. When she and Barry were playing tennis, all three labs—Lobo, TriStar, and Tanky—were watching intensely. If Barry or Sheila hit a tennis ball over the tennis-court fence, all three dogs would stand at attention. Barry or Sheila would call a dog by name to retrieve the ball. The other two would lie down in disappointment.

Chapter 15

KNOW THE SOURCE OF YOUR STRENGTH

Jim

One cannot endure what Barry has from his life's journey without reflecting on the virtues and values that enabled survival. When Barry speaks to groups or individuals, he always begins with the subject of American values. He considers this his legacy, and I am privileged to be a recipient of these stories.

Here are his reflective thoughts on the factors that contributed to his resilience. When we are faced with life-threatening situations, certain factors will enable us to survive. Faced with such a situation, what factors would help you survive? Where does your strength come from? What can you do to bolster that strength?

Barry

I do not consider my POW experience to be all that unique compared to the difficulties that some people endure daily. Of course, the six and a half years I was imprisoned in Vietnam were difficult ones, but the foundation to persevere was laid by all the experiences and relationships I had during my life prior to that time.

Despite losing six and half years of my life, I am blessed to have a loving family, friends, and colleagues who supported me before, during, and after my time in the Hanoi Hilton. I believe that each of us has an inner strength that allows us to deal with our difficulties in life. I also believe that those things that happened to us are not as important as our reaction to what happened to us.

As I share the factors that contributed to my resilience, I ask that you find a way to identify with these factors as you face adversity.

Nine Factors Contributed to My Resilience

I can think of nine primary factors that helped me get through six plus years as a POW without dying or going nuts.

1. Toughness

My toughness began with survival in an orphanage. The strains of survival in an orphanage will make you grow up quickly. You must manufacture your own fun if you want something to play with or do.

My orphanage experience lasted almost six years, and I'm sure it had a forever impact on my general attitude as a young boy and then later, as a man. My experience in the orphanage was to always anticipate that there would be a struggle. I carried that mind-set into my high school football years and beyond. I anticipated a battle and had to prepare for it. So, my foundation to fight was built in the orphanage, and it is still there.

In Hanoi, you didn't just go into the torture chamber one time; you were constantly in and out of that gosh damn torture chamber, depending on who you were and what they thought they could get out of you, or what they thought you'd be willing to surrender.

We made it a competition to stay in the torture chamber as long as possible to deny its use for a fellow POW. Only a bunch of Yanks would come up with that idea: "Let's have a competition to see who can stay in the torture chamber the longest." We tried to stay in the torture chamber as long as possible, in hopes that the Vietnamese torture program would just abate and go away.

We made everything a competition. We even began athletic competitions between one-man cells: "How many push-ups did you do without stopping?"

"How many did you do?"

"You go first."

"OK, I did fifty-seven."

"Well, I did fifty-nine."

"You go first next time. You're lying."

America's Vietnam POWs were constantly in and out of the torture chambers of North Vietnam, but it didn't mean we lost our sense of humor.

As POWs, we had toughness going into captivity, and that toughness was constantly being reinforced. When a POW was tortured, he worked his way through it and bounced back. My fellow POWs did a heck of a job. You knew you might be tested at any time. Giving up just wasn't in the cards. There was too much inspirational sacrifice going on all around us all the time by our fellow POWs.

2. My Family

I was adopted by a family that conducted themselves with the utmost integrity, possessed incredible character, used their God-given talents for good, and demonstrated their caring, respectful nature to everyone, every day. They inspired me to do great things for myself. I was not about to let them down. I carried the joy of life they had and the way they lived with me during my formative years, right on into the Hanoi Hilton prison.

3. My Comrades

The first time we were able to mingle with other POWs, I got to talk to CAG Stockdale and Colonel Robbie Reisner, both now deceased but never forgotten. They were incredible leaders who set the example for us all. These were the kind of people who surrounded me. I never ceased to be amazed at the caliber of the American Vietnam POWs I was fortunate enough to bump into, and what they were willing to do to help each other. They were a tough bunch of Americans because of what they valued about life and the values they carried in common into that hellhole.

We held some POWs in our arms who died from brutal torture, and another group who were driven insane and eventually came home in boxes after the war ended.

During Linebacker II, the final period of US involvement in the Vietnam War, we lost sixteen B-52s and a lot of electronic warfare officers. All B-52 crewmembers had the same chance of surviving a shoot-down, and the number of surviving crewmembers was consistent across all crew categories except EWOs (Electronic Warfare Officers). These men did not survive their shoot-downs in numbers consistent with their individual chance of survival. That suggests to me that some who survived the shoot-down and subsequent capture were retained because of their detailed nuclear and electronic warfare knowledge about the B-52 aircraft. Some may have gone to Russia or China. I can't prove any of that, but I am suspicious.

4. Character

Another principal value that I think played a major influence on all of us was the importance of character. That means doing the right thing when nobody's looking and doing the right thing when the heat is on and everybody is watching.

I was just amazed at the caring and respectful nature of all my colleagues in the prison camps of North Vietnam. That kind of character comes from how you were raised, your community, your family, and your country. You demonstrate character, confidence, a caring and respectful nature, and the ability to impassion and inspire those around you by your conduct, your actions, and your words.

At night, we would hear guys screaming from torture. That was the most disturbing thing that happened to me in Hanoi because I couldn't do anything about it. There were many opportunities to be inspired and to re-establish the importance of helping somebody in greater need than yourself.

I was amazed how my fellow POWS would jump to help those in greater need than themselves, no matter the consequences. If there was any chance that they could make a difference, they leaped into the breach—amazing, just incredible.

You'd be amazed at the amount of torture endured by America's Vietnam warriors. The North Vietnamese camp authority was no less astonished and stood in stark disbelief that all the American POWs would choose the torture chamber rather than provide them any form of cooperation. There were plenty of examples every day of somebody doing extraordinary things because their value system demanded it.

5. Traditional American Values

America's warriors do not seek praise and adulation for their service. Their fervent prayer is that our citizens would understand that a fulfilled life is not made possible by what you acquire unto yourself but what you give. And what you give will be determined by what you value about life, about living, about being.

To answer the question of why and how our veterans have never failed to serve our country with distinction, we need to understand the values they bring to every fight. I will illustrate those values from the story I know best: the American Vietnam POW story.

The most cherished value we Americans hold in common is out love of liberty. Its birthplace was the Greek city-state of Sparta. Now Sparta, unlike its cousin Athens, was not known for its edifices, its monuments, or it's great works of art. Indeed it left none of those things behind. It left much more!

In 480 BC, at the Battle of Thermopylae, King Leonidas and three hundred Spartan warriors held back one million invading Persians for three days in a narrow mountain pass in one of history's most memorable last stands. In that one battle, Spartan warriors championed the right of all men to be free and laid the foundation for liberty. For nearly two and a half centuries, America and our allies have been freedom's champion, and the sacrifice to safeguard the blessings of liberty continues to be secured by the shed blood of American warriors. The combat veteran knows that the cost of freedom is high, and the blessings of liberty are priceless.

But liberty is not just for Americans, our allies, and our friends. Liberty is a God-given natural right of all mankind. That is why I believe the young men and women serving in the armed forces of these United States today are living in a defining moment of history. Hopefully, their generations shall witness the last great battles among the forces of evil, the forces of totalitarianism, and freedom. Their challenge, of course, is global terrorism.

As you know, terrorists do not seek victory on the battlefield. Rather, they pursue their political objectives through fear and intimidation. They are a hidden enemy that attacks the innocent—and yes, they would prefer to use weapons of mass destruction. I share a belief, therefore, with many others that the challenge for today's generation is more difficult, more confusing, yes more dangerous than ever before.

America's warriors quickly learn that the desperate crushing environment of combat or a prisoner of war camp can destroy the mind and the body, but it cannot touch the values of a good heart and spirit. Our ancestors understood this very well.

They were deeply religious people whose life journey was filled with great trial and tribulation as they fought to gain—and then they fought again and again to maintain America's liberty. They did not have the luxury to adopt a value system that felt good, was fashionable, but would surely fail them in tough times. They quite naturally sought the wisdom of the ages carefully recorded in history, philosophy, and religious doctrine to provide to themselves and their nation the greatest opportunity to endure, indeed, to prosper. Then they enshrined those values into our Constitution and Bill of Rights, values that gave birth to the greatest expansion of human freedom and prosperity in the modern age, values that beat on in the DNA of every American heart longing to be reaffirmed.

America's warriors have always walked onto the battlefields of our nation's enemies, and some of us into the prison camps of our adversaries, with these values of our ancestors, and they have always brought us home with honor. Our experience in Vietnam was that kind of struggle.

In Vietnam, caring for one another was, for us, the right thing, the proper thing, the Christian thing to do. We did so naturally, instinctively, without forethought. In other words, our value system was on autopilot. It compelled us to act on one another's behalf, and thereby to survive. Tough times were no match for the power of traditional American values.

The founders of our republic held in common their love of freedom and the right to govern themselves. They were also willing to fight to the death to preserve these fundamental rights, and so were we. They were also in agreement that a corrupt and vicious people could never make the principles of self-government work. Yet today we find America, indeed the world, spinning in chaos. We are increasingly a divided nation quarreling over a multitude of important, sensitive, and contentious issues that effectively camouflage the greatest threat to our republic: a lack of wisdom and virtue in our elected leaders.

The armed forces of these United States of America is one of the most prestigious institutions in America, and for good reason. The conduct of our warriors on and off the field of battle is a reminder to every American that the profound ideas and principles upon which the greatest nation in human history was built are still there. They work the same way every time they are tried, and they are beckoning all of us to come home and reclaim the promise of America. The values of our ancestors were front and center in the dungeons of North Vietnam. If we weren't all in it together, it would be every man for himself—and it was not that way.

We were governed by our values to hang together and to help one another. Our greatest treasure was to help those in the greatest need. It was an instinct and action that did not require thinking. We just did it.

When I was in Hanoi, Admiral Stockdale shared a quote from Epictetus, the old Greek stoic philosopher: "Wish things were the way they are, and still carry on well."

My daughters, throughout their high school and college years, had that quote on their computer screen savers, flowing from right to left. Those gals are dynamite.

Where are the individuals in our community and in our institutions who champion character, competence, and being caring and respectful of everyone? You're going to have an influence on the people you meet in life. Depending on what your value system is, it will have a variable impact. It could be positive and uplifting, or it could promote a downtrodden state and victimization. I don't have time for that. You don't acquire a fulfilled life out of being a victim; you earn it by inspiring others to discover and develop their natural talents.

6. Confidence

Confidence played an important role as well. Whether faced with torture or the despair of not returning home alive, you must have confidence that by the grace of your faith, you can overcome whatever confronts you.

We had confidence in our families, our leaders, and ourselves that we would not be forgotten and that our loved ones and a grateful nation would fight to bring us home. This confidence made life worth living, allowing us to make it through each day, ready to confront what would happen to us in the future. Besides, helping our fellow POWs to survive was a critical and relentless task. War in the prison camps of North Vietnam was every day!

7. Education and Knowledge

Our academic background was important, too, because, as mentioned, the only toys we had in North Vietnam were our own brains. We had no pencils, no papers, nothing to exercise our thoughts. If you were caught with anything, you were going to the torture chamber. It was dangerous to try to make your own pens and pencils and communicate.

Many people think material things in life cause happiness, but exercising your mind, dreaming the dreams of children, and expanding your thinking all allow you to leave the harshness of your reality to a place that results in happiness. It is not what is happening to you that determines your lot in life, but how you think about it. Education and knowledge allow you to transcend yourself from where you are to places that are unimaginable otherwise.

8. Virtue

I promise you, virtue was everywhere in the prison camps of North Vietnam. You talk about sacrificing for the greater good of those about you. It was ongoing all the time, inspirational as the dickens. I was proud to be part of such a great bunch of Americans.

I travel all over the country speaking to various groups and organizations. Everywhere I go, I run into a lot of academicians, teachers, and so forth. I ask them, "How many hours on the principles and practices of liberty do you provide to your students over the course of a four-year education?" I would be hard-pressed to say I've ever received an answer much above zero. It should come as no surprise that if you walk away from virtue and wisdom and all that must transpire to make that happen, the survival of these traditional American values is seriously threatened.

I remind myself that, thankfully, one of the last great bastions of virtue resides in the hearts of the men and women who serve our country in uniform.

Civics was a wonderful course for me when I was in high school. The message of civics says, "Hey, we can't rule by whim." Law must govern us. Do we want to be a communal society or a people out there developing our God-given skills and applying them to enrich our lives and those about us? Where is the discourse on these issues today?

9. Faith

My parents instilled in me character; integrity; a deep, abiding love for our great country; and the importance of turning to our blessed Lord in times of need. Your enemies can try to break you physically, psychologically, and emotionally, but they can never take away your faith. It is a miraculous source of strength and hope, even in the darkest times of your life—*especially* in those dark times.

Why We Resisted: The Resistance Pyramid

For the first five years of the Vietnam War, the North Vietnamese government placed all of America's prisoners of war into individual solitary confinement cells with a twofold purpose: to separate us from one another, which was our strength, and to provide to their camp authority the opportunity to try to destroy our cultural bonds and heritage. Under these conditions, as you would anticipate, spontaneous, covert communications erupted.

These communications were difficult and dangerous, and our senior leaders were often out of that communication loop for months, if not years, at a time. If we made contact, we expected from them sound policy guidance, which they often had to provide on the spur of the moment. Eventually, our senior leaders were removed from our ranks and placed into a special punishment camp. We were left to fend for ourselves as individuals, cellmates, and small groups. Yet we still successfully resisted the efforts of the North Vietnamese camp authority to exploit us. The question is, why?

Col. Galen Cramer, a Vietnam prisoner of war and friend, provides an answer with what he calls the "resistance pyramid," shown here:

The Resistance Pyramid

Local resistance & self-defense

Tribal organization

Global information warfare

Financial resilience

Individual improvement

This pyramid was developed by Daryush Valizadeh, an industrial microbiologist by trade who left his career to travel the world and write books. Valizadeh explains why he developed this depiction of escalating levels of resistance: "There's a balance to be struck between maintaining our freedom (self-preservation) and enacting the change we want to see in our city or society. I've developed the resistance pyramid as a hierarchy of action to becoming a force that resists state or mob efforts to remove your liberties or displace you from your home. Lower levels on the hierarchy should be completed before attempting the higher levels."[37]

---

37   Roosh Valizadeh, "The Resistance Pyramid," Roosh Valizadeh's blog, April 11, 2016, https://www.rooshv.com/the-resistance-pyramid.

In the upper portion of the pyramid, you can see a variety of reasons that you might choose to resist exploitation. Some POWs resisted because of their training, heroic acts of their fellow POWs, or love of country. And would you believe, we had some Americans in North Vietnam who were absolutely terrific resisters because they were obstinate people. Do you know anyone like that? In other words, these Americans did not want to be told what to do by their legitimate senior ranking officers or NCOs. They darn sure didn't want to be told what to do by the North Vietnamese camp authority.

So what is the message?

If you happen to know someone who is in the military or headed in that direction whom you judge to be stubborn and pigheaded, these are the kinds of individuals who are appropriately nominated for the lead aircraft, the lead ship, or the point. They would probably make pretty decent POWs. There was, however, one fundamental, undergirding factor that buoyed up all others: the unwillingness of the individual to sacrifice his own personal reputation.

At Least Two Betrayed Their Comrades

I don't have firsthand evidence of any one POW's conduct throughout his experience, but as best as we can determine, almost all of America's Vietnam prisoners of war went into the torture chamber.

According to *The Washington Post*, eight Vietnam POWs were accused of collaborating with their North Vietnamese captors.[38]

When we came home, we filed charges against two of these individuals because it was our understanding that they were collaborating with the enemy. They tried to influence others to claim and to champion the idea that this was "an unjust war."

Admiral Stockdale, one of our senior ranking officers, an incredible human being, now deceased, and others in our POW leadership filed formal

---

38   Michael E. Ruane, "Traitors or Patriots? Eight Vietnam POWs Accused of with Collaborating with the North Vietnamese," *The Washington Post*, September 22, 2017, https://www.washingtonpost.com/news/retropolis/wp/2017/09/22/traitors-or-patriots-eight-vietnam-pows-were-charged-with-collaborating-with-the-enemy/?noredirect=on.

charges against those two individuals. Beyond that, as far as I know, everybody went to the torture chambers and refused to collaborate. Some went more often than others. The amount of torture you took depended on a variety of factors.

Those two who turned on our government and great nation tried to influence the other POWs who were all sitting in our 120-degree solitary-confinement cells. They had three meals a day of good food, exercise, basketball goals, and all kinds of privileges the rest of us did not have. We tried to change their attitude and bring them back into the fold. Admiral Stockdale got wind that the rank-and-file POWs had been watching these two guys and noted the quality of treatment they were getting while we were going to the torture chambers every other day. We were getting hostile about the idea. Word got back to Admiral Stockdale that if we were to get hold of those guys, we were going to take them out. He immediately fired a message through the POW system that said, "Now, hear this. It is neither a Christian nor American to drag a repentant sinner to his grave. I therefore do not want a day to go by that we don't make every effort to contact these two men and tell them to come home."

The truth of the matter is, the leadership tried their best to get these two guys to come back into the fold and be forgiven, but unsuccessfully. That's why formal charges were filed at the end of the war.

Imagine my surprise when President Carter later betrayed us:

During his 1976 presidential campaign, Jimmy Carter promised to pardon draft dodgers as a way of putting the war and the bitter divisions it caused firmly in the past. After winning the election, Carter wasted no time in making good on his word. Though many transplanted Americans returned home, an estimated 50,000 settled permanently in Canada.

Back in the US, Carter's decision generated a good deal of controversy. Heavily criticized by veterans' groups and others for allowing unpatriotic lawbreakers to get off scot-free, the pardon and companion relief plan came under fire from amnesty groups for not addressing deserters, soldiers who were dishonorably discharged or civilian anti-war demonstrators who had been prosecuted for their resistance.[39]

Although some supported this decision by President Carter, my fellow POWs and I saw it as a betrayal of all we gave to defend this country. I cannot see the wisdom in doing this, and I don't think I ever will.

Change Behavior to Change Values

During a question-and-answer (Q&A) session following a presentation I gave recently, an audience member asked me, "How does someone change what he or she values about life, about living, about being?"

My years upon this Earth have convinced me that the gateway to changing values is to change behavior. From life's experiences, you know you can change someone's behavior with force, pain, and motivational gimmicks, but for how long? Temporarily—ask my Mama. As a little boy, I received two to three switchings per week. Every time she administered one of those, I changed my behavior—temporarily.

Here is what my Mama missed.

If you want to change someone's behavior permanently, you have no choice but to transform their *attitude*. But the only way to transform attitude is through inspiration. To do so, according to the Roman philosopher Cicero, you must encounter a vision that turns the soul—a vision with the power to change who you are and how you think forever.

My two daughters were blessed at birth with many talents and abilities. As they grew into adulthood, we continuously sought to inspire them to develop their gifts with this admonition, "Your Creator has given you much to enrich the lives of those about you, to bring you peace and joy you can neither stop nor measure. So why would you ever give less than the full measure of God's blessings to every soul you are privileged to touch? Never fail to give them your best."

So, what are some sources of profound inspiration? Well, first of all, literature. As a young boy, my mom tried in vain to encourage me to read. Her

---

39 "President Carter Pardons Draft Dodgers," History.com, https://www.history.com/this-day-in-history/president-carter-pardons-draft-dodgers.

favorite tactic was to trap me at the front door on Saturday mornings as I headed out to play. She would entice me to read with pictures from a book showing a kid on a raft and whitewashing a fence. My response was always the same: "Mom, I have two choices. I can sit down and read this story about this little boy who clearly does not know how to make a raft and can't paint, or I can go out and live life. Mom, I prefer to live life."

Here's what I missed. You cannot live long enough on this Earth to gather together the experiences required to convert in full measure the totality of your raw talent to skill. You must therefore depend heavily on the experiences and insights of others who are demonstrably skilled in those areas in which you seek to excel. The treasures of their Life's work are buried in the written word, waiting to transform your life.

Relationships are another source of profound inspiration. You are well served to seek relationships with men and women of undisputed moral virtue, who are competent in what they do, caring and respectful of everyone, and visionary.

Finally, institutions you affiliate with may also transform your life. America's combat warriors learn quickly not to focus on the final score, but only on the play at hand, that you cannot be a American warrior of one, a POW of one, a wounded warrior of one, or anything else of one and have much of a chance to prevail and prosper.

Joining the correct group can be a game changer for your physical and emotional well-being due to the help you will receive from one another. Conversely, your spiritual well-being, your sense of inner peace, and personal contentment will not be dependent on the help you receive, but the help you are willing to give. The right institutions will embrace these principles as an important part of their culture because their faithful execution will best assure the inspired behavior and support we owe one another, our families, our community, and our nation.

The Only War America Hasn't Won

The Vietnam War, fought from 1954 until 1975, is the only war the United States ever lost. The conflict pitted the communist government of North Vietnam and its allies in South Vietnam, known as the Viet Cong, against the government of South Vietnam and its principal ally, the United States. the war was also part of a larger regional conflict (the Indochina wars) and a manifestation of the Cold War between the United States and the Soviet Union and their respective allies.[40]

As previously mentioned, on January 27, 1973, the Paris Peace Accords were signed, officially ending the American war in Vietnam. One of the prerequisites for, and provisions of, the accords was the return of all US prisoners of war (POWs). On February 12, 1973, the first of 591 US military and civilian POWs were released in Hanoi and flown directly to Clark Air Force Base in the Philippines.[41]

It was agony for all of us. No single POW could ever witness all the events that happened during the Vietnam War or interview all the former POWs. Hundreds of us are scattered all over the world, fully engaged with the challenges and blessings of life.

In 2000, former Vietnam POW John Hubbell wrote a book called *POW: A Definitive History of the American Prisoner-of-War Experience in Vietnam, 1964–1973*. That is the most comprehensive document I'm aware of that has been written about the Vietnam POW experience, in my opinion. The hardcover version contains 663 pages. Another thorough account of this subject is *Honor Bound: American Prisoners of War in Southeast Asia, 1961–1973* by Stuart I. Rochester and Frederick T. Kiley, published in 1999.

But truthfully, all books fall short of describing the entire POW experience in its totality. All we can do is share what we went through. And that's one of the purposes for this book. We can never forget the incredible courage our servicemen and women, especially the prisoners of war have demonstrated in fighting to preserve our American values.

I am very concerned about what's going on in America today. It seems like we have fewer and fewer people championing the principles and practices of liberty.

---

40 Ronald H. Spector, "Vietnam War," *Encyclopedia Britannica*, last updated November 14, 2018, https://www.britannica.com/event/Vietnam-War.

41 Adrian R. Lewis, "Vietnam War POWs and MIAs," *Encyclopedia Britannica*, undated, https://www.britannica.com/topic/Vietnam-War-POWs-and-MIAs-2051428.

Telling Our Story

If I had to pick a single individual who would do the best and most comprehensive job of telling the story of America's Vietnam prisoner of war experience, it's John M. (Mike) McGrath. He is the historian for our POW organization, NAM-POWs, and served as president twice. Mike also is the author of the book *Prisoner of War—Six Years in Hanoi.*

As a young US Navy pilot, Mike was captured in 1967 after being shot down over Vietnam. He is a self-taught artist, and in his book, he captures with stark detail the brutality of our existence in the North Vietnamese prison camps.

Here's what Mike would tell you: when we came home, we were besieged by people who wanted to hear the story of Vietnam, the POW camps, and so forth. Every time we attempted to do so, we were confronted and viciously attacked by two groups: Hollywood celebrities and politicians.

Each of us had a peephole that revealed our individual story of the gut-wrenching truth of the Hanoi Hilton and how it all unfurled. The magnitude of the story and the message to America will only be revealed when all the peephole pieces are assembled. The urgency of this effort is exacerbated by the death of some of our most influential and important leaders.

We're getting old. As we die, the story dies. Mike has firsthand knowledge of our unsuccessful fight so far to create a film that comprehensively tells the Vietnam POW story, which is far-reaching.

Our story involves Russians, Chinese interrogators, and torture programs by the Cubans. It's a fascinating story. You wouldn't have to elaborate or exaggerate on anything, and you'd still have everybody sitting on edge of their chairs every night, waiting for the next episode. Hopefully someday, somebody will realize the value of talking about how the American POWs survived the experience. There is an enormous number of incredibly important messages that should be revealed and debated.

All the pieces of the puzzle are captured in detail in the extensive debriefings our Vietnam POWs accomplished upon our return. Those debriefings should be declassified and made available to authenticate and guide this profoundly important chapter in American History. Issues to overcome would include privacy, national security, and blowback from those implicated.

I urge you to support films that contrast the brutality of the Hanoi Hilton with the power of traditional American values.

Chapter 16

CONSTANTLY REINVENT YOURSELF

Jim

One of the hallmarks of Barry's life is that he constantly reinvents himself, as you will see from the number of different transitions he made and continues to make. He accomplishes these with the same resolve and focus that got him through his days as a POW. Each time I speak to him, he shares with me a new triumph in his life as he focuses on how he can make a difference in his and other people's lives.

He is an inspiration to all of us who think that life ends at sixty years old or at retirement. In his case, the end of one pursuit is just another stepping stone to find additional opportunities to excel.

Barry

A friend of mine, Ray Becker, felt that I would make a good financial advisor for First Command Financial Planning. He recommended that I meet with senior people at First Command for an interview. Specifically, Ray thought I would do well supporting US Army personnel assigned to Fort Leavenworth Military Installation even though I was a retired Air Force officer.

Jumping Right In

I retired from active duty on September 30, 1984. The next day, October 1, 1984, I put on a suit and went to work for a financial services company as a registered representative and agent doing personal financial planning.

My mentor and the person who convinced me to work with First Command was Ray Becker. Ray started with the company in its early years and continued for a thirty-five-year career. I met Ray while I was still on active duty at the Army's Command and General Staff College in Fort Leavenworth, Kansas. Although it is an Army school, Air Force and Navy instructors complemented the staff of Army instructors, which is typical for higher-education military schools. I was an Air Force instructor for tactics.

Ray was an outdoorsman and hunter, like me. Ray also had a lot of land for hunting. It was fortuitous that I met Ray early in my career and was able to develop a strong relationship with him.

I tell financial advisors all the time, "If you want to make progress with someone, you've got to give them the opportunity to take the measure of you. Give them an opportunity to evaluate you, in terms of your character, your competence, your nature, in terms of being caring and respectful, and your capacity to be visionary. Being visionary is important because people don't respond emotionally to *facts*. They respond emotionally to *stories*."

The company I went to work for, First Command, had an onboarding process for new hires that was referred to as VIP. This was an opportunity for the senior executives to interview the candidates to find out their suitability for a career in financial services.

This process gave managers an opportunity to instill the company founder's values and culture in the new candidates. There was truly a family atmosphere of cooperation and helping each candidate receive the start that a new entrepreneur needed.

Because advisor compensation was totally through commissions, new candidates for jobs had to have a certain amount of money to start. Retired military personnel fit in well with the culture and generally had the financial wherewithal to make the transition. I was an ideal candidate for this career, but I had no experience in sales. This was true for most who attended VIP, so it was especially important for management to gather a lot of data on new candidates so they could make a good decision in accepting a new hire. The process took almost two days before candidates were fully vetted. Spouses were encouraged to attend, so they also knew what to expect. A family atmosphere existed.

When Sheila and I returned home, I turned to her and said, "What do you think?"

Her response was, "It cannot be a mistake to go to work for a company with so many great Americans."

Boy, is that true. Then she asked me, "How long is it going to take for you to come up to speed?"

I said, "Well, it depends on whether or not I piddle."

She said, "There is no way that's going to happen. You go to work. I'll take care of the home front. You're not a prairie chicken. You're an eagle."

Straight to the Top, and Fast

I attribute any success that I did enjoy primarily to my sweetheart, my support team, and to the quality of the people who worked for the company. That support was a game changer.

When I went to work for First Command, I arrived with $6,000 worth of computers. Back then, corporate America and computers were just getting to know one another. At that time the founder of our company banned personal computers because in those early years, computers were often viewed as time wasters, glorified game machines.

When I began work, I asked Rich Giles, my district manager, how much production I needed to qualify my family's attendance to the upcoming annual sales meeting? At that time, the qualification year was already 2/3rd old. Rich looked up at me and said, "Bridger, go back to work. Do not ask silly questions. You just started. Leave." So I left. April came along, and I asked Rich again, "How much production credit do I need to go to the sales meeting?" He looked at me and said, "I'm not going to tell you again. Go back to work."

When June came around, I walked into Rich's office and said, "How much do I need?

This time he paused, smiled and said $125,000 in production. I made it. My family went to the sales meeting. First Command also created a special award that year for me called the "Mach Buster of the Year" award. With the incredible support of my wife and team we made the next to the highest award level that year in five months.

During the CEOs sales meeting presentation he said, said, "It has come to my attention that there are advisors in our company, who are using computers. And if I find out who you are, you will be out of this company by the close of business today."

Rich nudged me with his elbow and said, "You bought a typewriter."

I said, "OK."

About three years later, I went to the sales meeting. As I sat in the audience, the company CEO said, "It has come to my attention that we actually have advisors in this company who don't have computers. If I find out who you are, you'll be out of this company by close of business today."

When I went to work for the company, no one had white boards of any kind. I installed a six-foot by seven-foot white board on day one My military background as a briefer had demonstrated that the efficacy of this readily available, inexpensive tool that was generally unmatched to clarify critical issues.

Also, in those days no one did a thorough analysis of a client's budget, which I referred to as a "budget scrub." So I created a customized budget sheet to do budget scrubs. Today, you find personal computers, white boards, and computer-based budget scrubbing throughout the company. The tools that made such great sense to me on my first day of work are now commonplace in the company.

Jim

I ran the training program for First Command when Barry was in his first few years as a financial advisor.. Barry was so passionate about assisting families based on all the experience he had that his appointments sometimes lasted up to four hours.

One day, when we were relaxing after a video shoot, Barry turned to me and said, "You've done a lot for me. What can I do for you?"

I said, "Barry, there's one thing you can do for me, but it will be for you, too. You've got to get your appointments to one hour."

Barry did not agree. He said, "Oh no. No, no. There's so much I've got to tell them."

I said, "Barry, you can make so much more and effect so many more people if you will just get these appointments to one hour."

He looked at me as if it would never happen. Despite the fact that he disagreed with me, Barry focused on doing just what I asked. I am not sure whether he ended up at an hour or not, but he significantly decreased the time and continued to do well, despite spending less time with clients.

Barry was the top producer for the company multiple times. By the time we had this conversation, it was likely 1988. He won the top honors three years in a row—1988, 1989, and 1990. He did even better when he cut down the time he spent with clients because he had more time on his hands to work with more clients and to take some time off to help his family. As a result, he was happier and more successful.

Barry would not take no from a client. He knew the devastating effect on families if his mostly military family clients ever faced the kind of loss that Barry experienced in Vietnam without having the proper insurance in place. Barry would not let anyone shirk familial responsibilities. Barry met with one guy at least a dozen times before he said yes. He said, "Damn it. I'll sign."

Rich Giles also asked Barry to shorten his meeting times. He said, "Barry, you're really good, and your clients obviously love you, respect you, and believe everything you tell them. But you use too many words. You use ten when you could use two."

Barry's reply was, "But it sounds so good coming out of my mouth."

Barry
My Third Career as a Professional Speaker

Reinvention has always been a part of my life, but mastering a new skill takes many hours. I subscribe to Malcolm Gladwell's 10,000 hours that he mentions in his bestselling book, *Outliers* to become accomplished in a trade. After serving as a successful advisor from 1984 through 2004, my company asked me to become a spokesperson, for First Command, an Ambassador at large. I don't mind traveling and speaking, so I accepted.

When I came home in 1973 and back into the fighter squadron business, everybody was asking me to speak. I accepted all requests.

When you talk that much, it's like learning to play the guitar. Eventually, you might learn how to play it a little bit. Understandably, I became a better presenter from the sheer number of times I was asked to speak.

My favorite part of making a presentation is connecting with the audience. I want them to be emotionally impacted by my message.

Recently, an admiral came up to me at Hill Air Force Base in northern Utah and said, "I want you to know your presentation blew me away. You have got to go to northern Virginia and give this presentation. I will arrange it. Will you come?"

Another time, when I made a presentation to World War II, Korean, and Vietnam veterans, a young man came up to me and said, "I can't tell you how much I wish that I could give a presentation the way you do, the way you inflect when you speak. You're amazing."

I replied, "Put in your ten thousand hours developing your skills as a public speaker, and you'll be amazed at the power of your delivery."

I speak to a lot of current and former members of our armed forces. Sometimes, they approach me to talk and end up crying on my shoulder. This is tough for both of us, but it's almost impossible for me to do something that would be beneficial for them in a short moment. In the past, I tried to comfort them by saying, "Look, things are going to get better."

But now I encourage them to seek out those who are in greater need than themselves and support them. When you help somebody who's having a tougher time than you are, you won't believe what it's going to do for you. I saw that every day in Hanoi. You don't have to know the right answer all the time. You must care, and it has to show.

My Speaking Circuit

I'm always thanking the Lord for what I know is happening. And then I see proof of it. For example, I have no doubt that since 1973 I have been talking, without letting up, to all kinds of audiences, worldwide. I've spoken to academicians, universities professors, ROTC instructors, corporate boards, high school and college students, academies, military organizations etc. The power and value of my message is fundamentally better than it was.

All this time, the Lord had me serving as an instrument, as an apostle. Here are the three things I pray about all the time:

1. First, I pray to be a better person. I say to the Lord, "Thank you for helping me become a better person. Reveal unto me the man you want me to be."

2. I also thank Him for revealing to me raw talents I did not know I possessed. Have you ever stopped to consider the millions of people born to this Earth with incredible talents, who live a long life and die, never knowing the blessings they possessed? Converting raw potential to skill has brought me an enormous amount of joy. Four years ago, my Messiah declared to me, "Your skill as a public speaker is established, but I also gave you the talent to sing. I want you to develop both." So I pray that I shall continue to work hard, with passion and inspiration, to speak and sing as well as the Lord created me to do it, and give it all back to him.

3. Finally, I thank the Lord for letting me walk this Earth and share His views through me about life, about living, about being, about faith, and about the multitude of things I'm privileged to talk and sing about.

This collection represents only about one-third of the coins, plaques, and other memorabilia I have received from my speaking engagements over the years.

Reinventing Myself as a Songwriter and Singer

When something monumental happens in our lives, we can choose to either let that experience define us or continue to evolve beyond that experience. I do not want to be known simply as a former prisoner of war. So I have reinvented myself several times—first, as I described, by completing a successful career as a financial advisor then by becoming a prolific public speaker, and finally as a singer and songwriter.

I cannot just stop and look back; I need to move forward. That is why I have continued my life's journey by learning how to play the guitar from a CD that I play on a computer.

The instructor says, "If you're serious about learning to play the guitar, you have to practice these scales that I teach you today at least fifteen minutes a day, five days a week." I am averaging about six hours a day every day. I figured, "I think I can put this whole thing together maybe in two weeks." That dogged determination is how I approach everything in my life.

At the time of this book, I have 6,000 hours, roughly, of hard work into learning how to sing and play the guitar. The challenge for me, since I could do neither before setting off on this journey, is to engage the services of someone who can truly help me in the singing arena—a voice coach, a vocal coach. I keep putting that off because I am experiencing on going improvements in the quality of my voice. Feedback from friends validates my vocal improvement.

My interest in singing began about five years ago, when I typed into a computer how to sing? I was immediately flooded with 200 years' worth of information. I discovered David Jones who is an opera singer and instructor, living in England. He is an incredible writer who writes about how to sing with the same power that the Russian author, Dostoevsky, wrote about the Russian winter. In other words, he speaks little, says much. Regarding the Russian winter, Dostoevsky was so powerful in his narrative and rhetoric that after you read the third page, you had to put a blanket around you because you were so damn cold. That's how powerful David Jones's word choices are. He writes in one of his articles, "Would you like to know why you can't sing worth a flip?"

I said, "Yes."

He said, "Turn the page."

I turned the page. There was an X-ray of a larynx, a young man's voice box with two little lines. He said, "Look at these two little lines, and notice where they end. They point to what looks like two little BBs, one on each side of the throat. Those are supposed to be muscles. Those muscles don't exist. They're like peas. This kid who came to see us, whose X-ray we took of his voice box and who wanted to learn to sing, has no chance of holding a tune with no muscularity in his throat. You must develop these muscles, just like your biceps, to be physically strong. In other words, you've got to put your voice box through a weight-lifting program, just like your arms and legs. So that is how I am learning to sing.

I continue to improve and fantasize that I will one day play the guitar and sing like the pros. When you put your mind to it, practice hard, and focus each day, you will amaze. This is a good rule for life.

It'll take every bit of about five to six years of your life to be able to have a capability to read music and play it on the guitar, at least that, and I'm in my eighties. I figure I've got at least twenty more years, so I should be in good shape. I'll put in my six or so years, and then I think I'll get an electric guitar and do something else.

Who Knows What's Next?

What am I going to do with my musical career? Sometimes when I try to play my guitar, I say to myself, "I should give this up." Instantly, something in my body says, "You could live to be a hundred and three, and you need only five years to learn to play well. What's the problem?"

Those who play say, "Slow is smooth. Smooth is fast." But you want to learn faster, and you're always pushing too hard. If I'm trying to play a note, I should go no faster than I can read the note, translate the note to a letter in my head, convert in my head which string the note is on, and translate from where that string is to where the note is on that string.

Although I try to teach myself, a coach can get me there faster, so I will hire one eventually. I am also trying to become a decent singer. So, what am I trying to achieve in my musical career? My ultimate goal is to develop a skill set that would allow me to take whatever the Lord gave me, in terms of raw talent, intellect, and hard work—just me and my guitar, connecting with the audience. I've also thought about starting a singing competition program to compete with *America's Got Talent* called *America's Old Fogies've Got Talent*.

We'll kick their behinds.

I like to stay active. To some degree, you don't want to wait too long and be idle too long, no matter where you are in your life. You really need to stay engaged in some intelligent way with the press of life.

I gave a presentation at the over-fifty-five community north of Orlando called The Villages. People there are incredibly active. In the front row were four people who were ninety-five to one hundred years of age. I was humbled to speak to that group. One of them had earned the Congressional Medal of Honor and was an ace in Korea. Sitting there looking at those old boys. I said, "Guys, you all need to be doing the talking."

One of them said, "We ain't going to do no doggone talking. Go."

Chapter 17

LIVE BY YOUR VIRTUES AND VALUES

Jim

As previously mentioned throughout this book, Barry is extremely grateful to those who gave him purpose in life. Like many of us, Barry searched throughout his life to find real meaning for others and for himself. He strongly believes in living life according to one's virtues and values.

Before we can do that, we must define what our virtues and values are because they will influence how others know us. What virtues and values define who you are? Those who come after you will be inspired by things you've done in a virtuous manner and hopefully, they will follow your lead.

Barry

As soon as the Bridger family in Bladenboro, North Carolina, adopted me, I was immediately in Sunday School, prayer meetings, church services, and all that you could imagine for someone who grew up in a devout Christian family.

To my young eyes, the Bridgers were really good people. They were kind and considerate, they told the truth; they talked about the truth; and they were very smart, competent, and into learning. They worked hard. I observed all of these characteristics, even as a young six-year-old.

I was immediately thrust into the dead center of a small, very close, very religious community with a variety of denominations and sects represented. That's where it began. "Raise a child up in the way he should go, and when he is older, he shall not depart from it. That was the way it worked in the Bridger family.

Aristotle said, "Any man can obtain virtue if he has a guide."

I had a heck of a guide in the Bridger family. All the Bridgers and all the people in my small community were guides. There was no way not to see the path; it all lit up, based on how they all felt and what kind of people they were. This didn't happen overnight. Obviously, I had to evolve because I came out of a "me first" orphanage experience. But suddenly, I was being told that I should be last, and my neighbor should be first.

God Has a Plan for Each of Us

When I was in the orphanage, no one was talking to me about values, virtue, ethics, or character. I had no one to talk to except Billy, and he didn't know anything about values, either.

During those years, the Lord was doing all the work. I wasn't saying, "Lord, thank you for helping me become a better person." I hadn't gotten there yet. But He was taking care of Billy and me.

The Lord has plans for all of us. He certainly had plans for me—I have no doubt. And He still does. He's going to take care of His people. And you can spend your time thanking Him for it because you don't have to ask.

For me, the growth of my faith began in earnest when the Bridger family adopted me. They were Southern Baptists. We went to prayer meeting every

Wednesday night, every Sunday, and every religious holiday. It was a way of life. I was in the choir, youth groups, Bible studies, and Vacation Bible School. We had religious activities, picnics, and hayrides all the time. There weren't many people in Bladenboro, so everybody knew everybody well. The church was a prominent part of the life of my hometown.

I got to know all the people who were coming to the church when I was a very young kid, six or seven years of age. I was able to make a judgment about those people and my adoptive family. And every time I made that judgment, everybody had the same attitudes. They were all filled with character, gracious, and humble. They had all those same qualities that my adoptive family had, and I really liked what I saw.

My family obeyed the principles that are so important in creating a life worth living. That is, character. They had it in spades. They told the truth when *nobody* was looking. They told the truth when *everybody* was looking, and the heat was on. But they also were caring and respectful of everyone, and I observed all of this. They were competent in everything they did and took great pride in working hard to develop their skills.

At six years of age, my eyes were wide open, watching all this activity transpire. And then finally, my family was inspirational. They inspired me to do my best and not to be an 85-percenter. They constantly said, "You're better than that. You can do better than that." As I watched the family that I was adopted into conduct their daily lives and how they interacted with our neighbors and our relatives and friends and so forth, I could not help but be profoundly and positively impacted by what I saw.

My wife, Sheila and I have deep roots in faith. Sheila grew up Catholic, and I grew up Baptist. Sheila and I brought both our daughters up to love the Lord. Now they are instilling in their children a love for the Lord, prayers, Bible verses, and Christian songs.

During my life, there have been seven or eight "A-ha!" moments that were so profoundly impressionable on me that I literally dropped to my knees in tears.

One of those moments was when I met Sheila.

Our faith grew considerably once she and I married and had children. We were trying to be good role models for our girls so that they would see in us the same kinds of characteristics we saw in our own families. So it was natural for us to become members of the church, engage with the church, and do things that were church-oriented, like taking the girls to Vacation Bible School.

It was important for Sheila and me to represent character and competence, a caring and respectful nature, being visionary, and being able to impassion our girls to do the best they could in any endeavor they undertook.

We all do some bad things. We all need redemption and transformative grace from time to time, and we will receive it if we ask. The Lord knows what we need.

Pray Unceasingly, and Follow the Lord's Guidance for Your Life

I am becoming increasingly aware of two things.

The first is the importance of praying unceasingly. I do not believe that anyone can pray to God almighty unceasingly and not be changed. It will happen.

Keep praying. The Lord will act in His own and good time. He wants to hear you say, "Thank you for helping me become a better person." He doesn't want you to say, "Would you please make me a better person?" He's already hard at work doing it, so why don't you just thank Him for it?

I pray unceasingly. It doesn't matter where I am. I'll bet I pray twenty times a day. I'll go fishing, I'll catch a crappie and say, "Lord, I want to thank you for this crappie. And I want to thank you for the two big ones I'm going to catch next."

Months ago, I was out fishing brush piles in about 20 feet of water and got hung up. I always take the Lord fishing with me, so I said, "Here! You get it out." So God took the pole and started pulling on it. He couldn't get it unstuck. I laughed and said, "Give me that pole. When you come down to your lovely Earth, you must abide by your own principles that govern every aspect of our lives. So you are no better unhanging this hook than I am. Give me back that pole."

I talk to Him like that all day long.

The second thing I am keenly aware of lately is the fact that I am on a journey that is being absolutely directed in a very powerful and rewarding way for me. I am always thanking the Lord for what I know is happening.

The Biblical Significance of Coffee

Recently, I walked into our kitchen, and Ms. Sheila, my sweetheart, was sitting at the kitchen table, as is her practice, looking out the big bay window at her birds and flowers and doing her Bible study, which she never fails to do.

I came into the kitchen rubbing my eyes because I had just awakened. I asked, "Is the coffee ready?"

She looked up from the table and said, "Oh, no. You'll have to make the coffee."

I said, "Uh, uh, uh, uh, uh. First person in the kitchen makes the coffee."

Sheila turned and looked at me, smiled, and said, "I have it on biblical authority that only the man makes the coffee."

I looked at her in absolute disbelief and said, "Oh, really? Would you mind showing me your biblical authority?"

"Come on over here."

So I walked over to the kitchen table. She opened up her Bible, and with her right index finger, she started tapping at the top right-hand corner of the page. It said "Hebrews." Sheila said, "See? He brews."

It got worse. Sheila said, "I have a whole chapter on this. Would you like to see page two?"

I was stunned. But finally, my brain kicked into gear and I said, "Sweetheart, I hate to inform you that you have the wrong King James Version. I have the correct one. I will go get it. It has an S in front of the H and says, 'She brews!'"

Sheila Uses Psychology on Me

Sheila is drop-dead serious about maintaining a spotless, beautiful home. For her, cleaning the house is a daily therapeutic ritual.

Imagine the consternation she experienced upon returning home after recent double knee-replacement surgery to take care of herself and her home at the same time. My contribution to household chores was to periodically mop the floors. We have a large ranch-style home with tile floors. The work required to mop the floors in our home is equivalent to cutting the grass on a football field. However, when I do something, I do it with a vengeance. I can mop with the best of them.

That day, I had planned to go fishing. As I was about to leave, Sheila said to me, "Honey, our floors need mopping, and I've been meaning to tell you I know no one who can dispute mopping skills with you. But you deserve a break. Go fishing?"

"I said, 'No, ma'am. I'm going to mop this house.'"

Earlier, I described how my brother, McRae, would set me up by praising me and then asking me if I wanted to do something I didn't love to do. Sheila does the same thing.

Faith at the Hanoi Hilton

My faith journey really took off when I walked into my adoptive family. And then it got a booster shot when I was shot down over Hanoi. Not only did I land in a place where there was justification for great trepidation, the communist rulers of North Vietnam were not nice. They were very cruel, and life was immediately and profoundly difficult in a lot of ways.

However, to counteract that, my faith journey took a sharp turn as I tuned in to the attitudes and the conduct of my fellow POWs. I was amazed and pleased to see that I was rubbing shoulders with people who had all the same qualities I had watched my parents demonstrate. They had tremendous character. They were incredibly competent in all kinds of things. They came from every walk of life.

Also, they were caring and respectful of one another, including their North Vietnamese torturers. Finally, they were big-time inspirational. They could impassion you in a lot of ways. I was absolutely pleased to be around such great Americans.

I didn't know of any atheists around me the whole time I was in Hanoi. Every evening, the senior ranking officer of a cellblock or building would say, "God bless" by coughing the letters GB instead of tapping them. *Cough cough—cough* equals G. *Cough—cough cough* equals B. Every night from cell to cell, the entire prison area would erupt in coughing "God bless."

Prayer occurred throughout the day, whenever we were able to do it. During the day, it was dangerous because guards were all over the place. I prayed all the time, and I think everybody else did, too. I had no reason to believe they didn't. We joined in individual prayer before we went to sleep.

Throughout our internment, we fought an ongoing battle for the right to worship openly in our rooms. And every time we attempted this, in the wee hours of the morning that followed, the North Vietnamese government would send in their storm troopers to crush the religious expression.

Chapter 18

CLOSING THOUGHTS

Jim

The following are Barry's thoughts and perspectives on a variety of important subjects pertaining to living life with wisdom, resilience, and humility.

Barry

Virtue: You Have to Learn It

My journey to virtue started as a child. I was like a guided missile that had no governor on it. I was doing whatever I wanted.

When I was a young adult, my mother once sat down and wrote a letter to me that expressed her concern that I was heading down the wrong path. She wanted me to start understanding that there were consequences to the choices I was making.

Here is what Mom's letter to me said. I have kept her original handwritten version all these years because it is priceless to me:

My dearest Barry! (Sat.)

With all the love in my heart I want to call your attention to a few things. Things I can't talk to you about without a tremendous argument. You may not know it but you aggravate [sic] my heart condition by your carelessness and by your inconsideration of us. Your neglect of us when you are away. We lost sleep about your failure to contact us on your trip to Sewanee and this week you went off without any word of when you would be back. Don't think we were not worried. Maggie cooked supper two nights and we had no reason but to look for you. I didn't mind you going to Chapel Hill from Wilmington but I did mind your going without telling us your plans. I didn't know you took your clothes with you. If you had only told us it would have saved us the anxiety of expecting you. It hurts, too, to think you have no more respect for our feelings, furthermore it is not good for us to be put in that position. It is also embarrassing when our friends ask where you are. I have to say, "I don't know" with a reply "You don't mean he went off without telling you." I don't think your attitude is at all complimentary to a fine boy like you. In fact we have decided home only means to you a place to eat and sleep. You never stay here long enough for us to even have a friendly conversation. It's a rush in and rush out as quickly as possible. I fear you are setting a pattern or habit for life that will follow you even when you get married and that will not work then. You can double-cross us now but then it won't work. The world can't offer you a thing that will compare with a happy home life of family devotion and companionship, when you have a home of your own. My prayer is that you will make a wife happy and be a loving father. My dreams will be fulfilled.

Mom

Back then, I rationalized by telling myself that I didn't think they would mind that I was doing the things I was doing. But that wasn't true.

She was right. I was animalistic. The way you get rid of that is with culture, and culture is a matter of values, ethics, and deeply held beliefs that are engrained as, the English Author, Malcolm Gladwell says in his book Outliers, over many thousands of hours. It takes about 10,000 hours for you to evolve into a different person. Loving parents and a loving community shape you.

I was also hard-headed as a bull. I had taken a lot of hits in the orphanage, and it didn't bother me if this happened or that, but it did bother my mom and dad because virtue meant a lot to them. I had no idea what virtue was because I just fought all the time. That's not virtue. It's the opposite. In other words, I had to obtain virtue. I had to learn it. It's passed from one generation to the next. It's not hereditary. Again, as Thomas Jefferson said, "Virtue is not hereditary...it must be earned, learned, continually cultivated, and passed from one generation to the next."

We look to the people in our homes, schools, and churches to fuel the fires of virtue, but today, those indispensable pillars of support are in serious decay. My adoptive parents were the right people to help me learn and adopt virtue.

My brother came out of the Second World War. Talk about virtue! Try flying combat in the South Pacific. He was a titan of virtue.

I learned much about virtue from my cellmates in Vietnam, including Mike Christian. He was an inspiration to me because he did not give up. His resilience and patriotism should inspire every one of us to love America deeply.[42]

The Importance of Reading

I was a terrible reader early in life. I likely never read a book, and had no desire to read a book, before I reached my fifties.

I was extremely energetic, and I could remember things that I heard without hesitation. I was consumed with the influence of words and actions of people everywhere I went, and I absorbed it like a sponge. I might as well have been

---

42 You can read about Mike Christian's experience as a Vietnam POW in an article titled "The Story of Mike Christian, American POW," on The Citizens Flag Alliance website at http://www.citizensflagalliance.org/stories/story-mike-christianvietnam-pow.

reading. In fact, I learned more than if I had been just reading because I had so many inputs. I just filed them away, and the evidence kept mounting that I needed to continue to go in the direction in which my parents lived their lives.

When Mom's letter hit me, I really had a spurt. I did start reading in my fifties, and I was amazed how much I would have learned if I had been a reader. My mom often said to me, "You need to read."

As I previously mentioned, Mom's favorite tactic to encourage me to read was to trap me at the front door on Saturday mornings as I headed out to play. She would encourage me to read with pictures from a book showing a kid on a raft and white-washing a fence. My response was always the same: "Mom, I have two choices. I can sit down and read this book about this little boy, who clearly does not know how to make a raft and can't paint, or I can go out and live life. Mom, I'd rather go out and live life."

I was insistent, but Mom was teaching me an important life lesson.

Here's what I missed. You cannot live long enough on this Earth to gather together the experience required to convert, in full measure, the totality of your raw talent or skill. I learned later in life that you must depend heavily on the experiences and the insights of contemporaries, past and current, who are demonstrably skilled in those areas in which you seek to excel. A treasure trove of wisdom is buried in the written word, waiting to transform your life. Don't follow my path.

The books that shaped my life were those of the Founding Fathers on the principles and practices of liberty. I am absolutely amazed at the wisdom of the Founding Fathers. When I read what they learned about communal economics vs. free-market capitalism I ask myself, "Why would we ever walk away from the blessings of free markets?"

You won't if you're part of an educated populous, but if you're not educated, you are fair game to be dragged in all kinds of crazy directions and reap all kinds of negative consequences.

Communal Economics

This country was founded based on freedom, individualism, and people having the opportunity to be successful in life. When the Jamestown colony formed in the New World, the occupants had an issue to deal with. How were they going to get through the winter? They said something like, "We need food, and we don't know how to deer-hunt very well. So, we've got to plant some crops."

As previously mentioned, what they decided to do was to create a communal economics system. They took some land and cleared it as a group and decided everybody would participate in planting for the harvest. Everybody would also participate in the harvest. Then everybody would get to eat together, and they'd all live happily ever after. Well, human nature took over. Instead of everybody showing up to plant for the harvest, a few showed up, but a lot of people said, "Why should I show up? I think I'll go fishing. They're going to plant all that stuff for us anyway." The harvest was weak, and people went hungry.

The following year, the people in the colony changed their approach. They said, "That communal economics thing didn't work well. So this time, we're going to assign everybody a plot of ground, and each person gets to plant their own plot." Guess what? Jamestown had an overabundance of food.

Free-market capitalism works because it is based on an understanding of human nature.

Legacy

Here is the legacy I want to leave to my family. I would remind them to live by this model: first and foremost, to obtain virtue, which means you sacrifice your own private approach to life for the greater good.

I would tell them it begins with character. I would say that character means you do the right thing when nobody's looking. Character says more than that—it says you do the right thing when everybody's watching and the heat is on.

But it's much more than that. You also must be competent. You must be skilled at what you do. Would you follow, for example, a wonderful, virtuous commander into combat who was incompetent in accomplishing basic combat tasks? No. So, not only must you have character, you must be competent. You must apply yourself to convert the raw talent the Lord has given you into a skill that you can use to help your neighbor.

You can't get by with just being of good character and being competent. You must be caring and respectful. The Japanese have a wonderful saying: "I will not let you help me if you don't respect me." I like that. You can't just have great character and be competent, caring, and respectful. You must also be able to inspire and impassion those around you. You must be visionary. The late Mother Teresa was once asked, "How do you do great things for God?"

She said, "You can't do great things for God, only little things done with great love." That is my guiding message to my grandkids.

Happiness

A lot of people ask how I was able to endure when I knew that I was going to be incarcerated for a very long time. They ask, "How did you reconcile your circumstances, considering what you had experienced prior to being captured by the North Vietnamese as a lifestyle? Wasn't it extremely difficult for you to sit there and reflect on the past and regret, in a deep and sincere way, your circumstances in the present?"

My response to that is it never crossed my mind. I was never unhappy while I was in prison. I was never sad, and I was as active as I could possibly be with the only toy that I had, my brain.

To occupy the time, I entertained myself, and of course all the POWs were busy as the dickens trying to help each other survive. My gosh, I laugh at President Trump's comment when he was referring to John McCain: "I don't like American warriors who get captured."

Well, doesn't he understand, bless his heart, that war in a POW camp is every day? It never stops. You don't get to go on liberty or take time off to relax. Every day, you are fighting to help somebody around you who's in worse circumstances than you. We spent our time helping each other, nonstop. It was relentless. I had friends who had toadstools growing out of their ears, others who were in enormous pain. Torture was everywhere, so we were running helter-skelter, here and there, trying to find ways to help one another relieve the pain and console those who were having a much tougher time than we were.

To keep us in good spirits, we also prayed a lot. Prayer was unceasing. That's what the Lord said in the Bible. He said, "Pray without ceasing" (1 Thess. 5:17).

CONCLUSION:
THE MEANING OF LIFE

"Happiness does not consist in pastimes and amusements
but in virtuous activities."
—Aristotle

Jim

What is the meaning of life as seen through Barry Bridger's eyes? To be of good and faithful service to others.

Barry says, "When you have figured out how to do that, you have now entered the world of virtue, which is a willing sacrifice of one's private interest to serve a greater need of community or of country. And to the extent I obey that as I just expressed it, I could not be more content, I could not be happier, and I could not be more optimistic and passionate."

Here are some thoughts about the meaning of life spoken by Barry Bridger.

———————

Barry

America's Vietnam POWs were incarcerated in six foot by six foot concrete cells for years. Our long, dark night of terror lasted for years. We were all alone with our thoughts and values. Our refuge was primarily our faith and our minds, which were filled with education, memories, and the power of traditional American values. We possessed everything we needed to endure the tough times of the Hanoi Hilton. God bless America!

In Vietnam, I solved more problems with *nothing* than I did with *something* because I had control of my mind, similar to what I had experienced as an orphan. We got to the point of doing so much with so little, we figured we could do everything with nothing. That's where the happiness factor comes in. That's why POWs were happy. I was never, ever sad. I wasn't sitting around crying because of my circumstances.

Another former POW, Charlie Plumb, starts his presentations by walking back and forth on the stage the same number of steps it took to walk around that small cell. Six steps by six steps give one a sense of the smallness of the cells. The cell was a small box with little or no provisions. POWs escaped the confinement through our minds. Thought allows you to leave what may be a terrible situation and to transport yourself to somewhere else that is much better and calmer.

No matter what your circumstances are, you can escape through your mind.

You also escape these circumstances with your memory. We walked into Hanoi with a huge reservoir of ideas and principles that we learned over time and relied on heavily. In addition to what my mind could help me do, I had that reservoir of memory that was sustaining. This reservoir was there despite being shot down at twenty-seven years of age.

Just as my curiosity carried me through having no toys at the orphanage, at age twenty-seven, I had enough knowledge and curiosity to carry me for six and half years without any provisions in the cell. You never know what you might face. That precious institution called "higher learning" plays a major role in helping people discuss, have debates, and engage in all the same discussions the Founding Fathers did. If you don't, from time to time, revisit the underpinnings of your life and your nation, you will lose them. Happiness comes from the inside if you allow it.

I had a spiritual connection with my fellow POWs and that crazy mess we went through in Vietnam. We were always sacrificing and looking out for one another. We had to. It's the only way we could survive.

This book, *The Spirit to Soar*, focuses on how to be successful despite what is happening to you. Throughout my life, my focus has been on success, regardless of my circumstances. I often think of those individuals who have it more difficult than me and those who are more blessed than I was in life. Both groups have opportunities to be successful in America, despite the differences in their circumstances.

I hope that by reading this book, you will see yourself and dig deep within yourself to find the courage to soar above those difficult circumstances that are inevitable in life. There was a team of people supporting me as I navigated the turbulent waters of the Hanoi Hilton. You also have people who are pulling for you, even though sometimes it may not be obvious.

With the appropriate amount of focus, energy, and dedication to a cause, you can do most anything.

Thanks for reading the book. I hope it gives you the strength you need to soar.

MORE ABOUT BARRY BRIDGER

From left: Deidra, Sheila, Barry, and Courtney Bridger.

Barry B. Bridger, a retired United States Air Force Lieutenant Colonel, is a native of Bladenboro, North Carolina. In 1963, he graduated from the University of North Carolina with a bachelor of science degree in mathematics and was commissioned as a 2nd Lieutenant through the ROTC program.

Following undergraduate pilot training in 1964, LtCol (Ret.) Bridger was assigned to the 43rd Tactical Fighter Squadron at MacDill Air Force Base, Florida, where he performed duties flying the F-4 Phantom.

In 1965, he completed the US Army parachutist training course at Ft. Benning, Georgia, and in 1966, he completed his first combat tour, flying missions in Vietnam. He returned to the United States, upgraded to Aircraft Commander in the F-4 Phantom, and returned for a second tour flying missions over North Vietnam. During his tours in Vietnam, LtCol (Ret.) Bridger accumulated more than two hundred combat flying hours and conducted more than seventy combat missions flying over North Vietnam.

On January 23, 1967, LtCol (Ret.) Bridger was shot down over the city of Son Tay, North Vietnam, by a surface-to-air missile. He was subsequently captured by the North Vietnamese and spent more than six years in prison.

Following his repatriation in March 1973, LtCol (Ret.) Bridger requalified in jet aircraft and was assigned to Seymour Johnson Air Force Base, North Carolina. While there, he served as an instructor pilot in air-to-ground combat and held positions of Flight Commander and Assistant Operations Officer.

He earned his master's degree in business administration from Central Michigan University in May 1977. In January 1978, he graduated from the Armed Forces Staff College in Norfolk, Virginia. He was then assigned as an Air Force representative to the US Army Command and General Staff College at Ft. Leavenworth, Kansas, where he served as a faculty member and instructor for about three years. He then was assigned as the chief of the Air Force wargaming division at Ft. Leavenworth.

In October 1984, LtCol (Ret.) Bridger retired after twenty-two years of service in the US Air Force. His awards and decorations include the Silver Star, Legion of Merit, Distinguished Flying Cross, Bronze Star Medal w/V device Purple Heart w/OLC, Meritorious Service Medal w/OLC, the Air Medal w/4 OLC, and the Prisoner of War Medal.

Following retirement from the US Air Force, LtCol (Ret.) Bridger began a twenty-year agent career with First Command Financial Planning, where he was a four-time Top Gun. He formerly served as First Command's Ambassador-at-Large and spoke to civilian and military audiences around the world.

He has been married to his "Super Wife," Sheila, for forty years, and lovingly refers to her as "Super Sheila." They have two married daughters and three grandchildren.

Barry Bridger's Military Awards

1. Silver Star Medal

The Silver Star is currently awarded by all branches of the US Armed Forces to any person who, while serving in any capacity, is cited for gallantry in action against an enemy of the United States while engaged in military operations involving conflict with an opposing foreign force, or while serving with friendly forces against an opposing armed force in which the United States is not a belligerent party.[43]

Barry's Silver Star Citation reads as follows:

> The President of the United States of America, authorized by Act of Congress, July 8, 1918 (amended by act of July 25, 1963), takes pleasure in presenting the Silver Star to Major Barry Bruton Bridger, United States Air Force, for gallantry and intrepidity in action in connection with military operations against an opposing armed force on 28 January 1967, while a prisoner of war in North Vietnam. Ignoring international agreements on treatment of prisoners of war, the enemy resorted to mental and physical cruelties to obtain information, confessions and propaganda materials. Major Bridger resisted their demands by calling upon his deepest inner strengths in a manner which reflected his devotion to duty and great credit upon himself and the United States Air Force.

2. Purple Heart Citation

This award, the modern form of the original Purple Heart established by Gen. George Washington in 1782, is conferred on any person wounded in action

---

43 "Silver Star Medal Criteria," Air Force's Personnel Center, August 3, 2013, https://www.afpc.af.mil/About/Fact-Sheets/Display/Article/421936/silver-star-medal/.

while serving with the armed forces of the United States. It is also awarded posthumously to the next of kin of personnel killed or having died of wounds received in action after April 5, 1917.

The Purple Heart is awarded for wounds or death as result of an act of any opposing armed force, as a result of an international terrorist attack or as a result of military operations while serving as part of a peacekeeping force.

3. Legion of Merit

This award is conferred on officers and enlisted men of the armed forces of the United States and on nationals of other countries who have distinguished themselves by exceptionally meritorious conduct in the performance of outstanding services since September 8, 1939, the date of the president's proclamation of the state of emergency that led to World War II. The Legion of Merit may be awarded for combat or noncombat services; in the case of American military personnel, if the award is for combat service, it is shown by the wearing of a combat V device.[44]

Barry's citation reads as follows:

> The President of the United States of America, authorized by Act of Congress, 20 July 1942, takes pleasure in presenting the Legion of Merit to Major Barry Bruton Bridger, United States Air Force, for exceptionally meritorious conduct in the performance of outstanding services to the Government of the United States as a Prisoner of War in North Vietnam from January 1967 to March 1973. His ceaseless efforts, by a continuous showing of resistance to an enemy who ignored all international agreements on treatment of Prisoners of War, in the extremely adverse conditions of the communist prisons of North Vietnam, demonstrated his professional competence, unwavering devotion, and loyalty to his country. Despite the harsh treatment through his long years of incarceration, he continued to perform his

---

44 "Legion of Merit Criteria," Air Force's Personnel Center, August 3, 2010, https://www.afpc.af.mil/About/Fact-Sheets/Display/Article/421937/legion-of-merit/.

duties in a clearly exceptional manner which reflected great credit upon himself and the United States Air Force.

4. Distinguished Flying Cross

This medal is awarded to any officer or enlisted person of the armed forces of the United States who shall have distinguished her/himself in actual combat in support of operations by heroism or extraordinary achievement while participating in an aerial flight, subsequent to November 11, 1918.[45]

Barry's citation reads as follows:

> The President of the United States of America, authorized by Act of Congress, July 2, 1926, takes pleasure in presenting the Distinguished Flying Cross to First Lieutenant Barry Bruton Bridger, United States Air Force, for heroism while participating in aerial flight as an F-4C Aircraft Commander near Hanoi, North Vietnam on 23 January 1967. On that date, while flying in a flight of four aircraft on combat air patrol, Lieutenant Bridger, despite a serious degradation of his own electronic defensive capability, elected to remain with his flight in order to afford the maximum possible flight protection in a hostile environment. The outstanding heroism and selfless devotion to duty displayed by Lieutenant Bridger reflect great credit upon himself and the United States Air Force.

5. Prisoner of War Medal

The Prisoner of War Medal is awarded to any person who was taken prisoner or held captive while engaged in an action against an enemy of the United States; while engaged in military operations involving conflict with an opposing armed force; or while serving with friendly forces engaged in armed conflict against an opposing armed force in which the United States is not a belligerent party. The person's conduct, while in captivity, must have been

---

45   "Distinguished Flying Cross Criteria," Air Force's Personnel Center, August 4, 2010, https://www.afpc.af.mil/About/Fact-Sheets/Display/Article/421931/distinguished-flying-cross/.

honorable. This medal may be awarded posthumously to the surviving next of kin of the recipient.[46]

Barry's citation reads as follows:

> Major Barry Bruton Bridger, United States Air Force, was held as a Prisoner of War in North Vietnam from January 23, 1967, until his release on March 4, 1973.

Education

Barry graduated from Sewanee Military Academy, Tennessee, in 1958, where he lettered in four sports and received awards as the Most Valuable Football Player and was voted one of the Most Outstanding Cadets in his senior year.

In 1962, he graduated from the University of North Carolina with a bachelor of science degree in mathematics. In college, he was a member of the Air Force ROTC, and upon graduation he was awarded his commission and went to flight training.

Barry and Sheila in 2019, fishing for sharks.

---

46 "Prisoner of War Medal Criteria," Air Force's Personnel Center, August 4, 2010, https://www.afpc.af.mil/About/Fact-Sheets/Display/Article/421934/prisoner-of-war-medal/.

ABOUT THE AUTHOR

Jim Petersen, PhD, CFP®, CLF®, ChFC®, CLU®, RICP®, WMCP®, CRPC®, CAP®, CASL®, AEP®, CPMBC, CPBC
CEO, Diversified Professional Coaching, LLC
President, Professional Business Coaches Alliance, LLC
jim@jlpeterseninc.com

Jim Petersen is the Chief Executive Officer and Founding Principal of Diversified Professional Coaching, LLC. As a former financial services executive, he is committed to leading a company that coaches business executives, leaders, advisors, and clients to pursue their financial goals and lifetime dreams by bringing sound business acumen, financial knowledge, and trustworthy advice to a lasting relationship with each person he serves.

In addition, Jim is the president and owner of the Professional Business Coaches Alliance, LLC, which is committed to training and supporting the future of professional business coaches. As a Professional Master Business Coach, Jim has expertise in training and coaching business coaches, executives, leaders, business owners, and those who want to take their businesses to the next level.

He entered the financial services industry in 1983 while continuing almost a twenty-two-year career in the United States Navy and United States Navy Reserve. He served as a submarine officer and retired with the rank of Captain (0-6). As a commissioned officer in the US Navy, he served on active duty as a nuclear submariner for seven years. His military expertise included many aspects of nuclear propulsion and submarine warfare.

At the end of 2020, Jim retired from the financial services industry, having served in multiple positions in both the field and the home office. A seasoned executive with more than thirty-eight years of experience in the investment and financial services industries, he is an expert in the fields of financial planning, retirement planning, and leading large financial-planning organizations.

Jim graduated from the United States Naval Academy with a bachelor of science degree, and he earned a master of science degree in management and financial services from The American College of Financial Services (TAC), King of Prussia, Pennsylvania.

On June 1, 2017, he became the first financial services manager to be awarded a PhD in financial and retirement planning from TAC. He is currently the Roger Hull/James S. Bingay Chair of Leadership at TAC, teaching a variety of courses in the graduate school.

A free ebook edition is available with the purchase of this book.

To claim your free ebook edition:

1. Visit MorganJamesBOGO.com
2. Sign your name CLEARLY in the space
3. Complete the form and submit a photo of the entire copyright page
4. You or your friend can download the ebook to your preferred device

Morgan James
BOGO™

A **FREE** ebook edition is available for you or a friend with the purchase of this print book.

CLEARLY SIGN YOUR NAME ABOVE

Instructions to claim your free ebook edition:
1. Visit MorganJamesBOGO.com
2. Sign your name CLEARLY in the space above
3. Complete the form and submit a photo of this entire page
4. You or your friend can download the ebook to your preferred device

Print & Digital Together Forever.

Snap a photo

Free ebook

Read anywhere

CPSIA information can be obtained
at www.ICGtesting.com
Printed in the USA
JSHW011959080822
28989JS00002B/4/J

9 781631 956515